QUEERING MARRIAGE

Families in Focus

Series Editors
Anita Ilta Garey, University of Connecticut
Naomi R. Gerstel, University of Massachusetts, Amherst
Karen V. Hansen, Brandeis University
Rosanna Hertz, Wellesley College
Margaret K. Nelson, Middlebury College

Katie L. Acosta, *Amigas y Amantes: Sexually Nonconforming Latinas Negotiate Family*

Anita Ilta Garey and Karen V. Hansen, eds., *At the Heart of Work and Family: Engaging the Ideas of Arlie Hochschild*

Mary Ann Mason, Nicholas H. Wolfinger, and Marc Goulden, *Do Babies Matter? Gender and Family in the Ivory Tower*

Jamie L. Mullaney and Janet Hinson Shope, *Paid to Party: Working Time and Emotion in Direct Home Sales*

Markella B. Rutherford, *Adult Supervision Required: Private Freedom and Public Constraints for Parents and Children*

Barbara Wells, *Daughters and Granddaughters of Farmworkers: Emerging from the Long Shadow of Farm Labor*

QUEERING MARRIAGE

Challenging Family Formation
in the United States

KATRINA KIMPORT

RUTGERS UNIVERSITY PRESS
NEW BRUNSWICK, NEW JERSEY, AND LONDON

3-19-14
ww
$25.95

Library of Congress Cataloging-in-Publication Data

Kimport, Katrina, 1978–
    Queering marriage : challenging family formation in the United States /
Katrina Kimport.
        pages cm.—(Families in focus)
    Includes bibliographical references and index.
    ISBN 978–0-8135–6222–3 (hardcover : alk. paper)—ISBN 978–0-8135–
6221–6 (pbk. : alk. paper)—ISBN 978–0-8135–6223–0 (e-book)
    1. Same-sex marriage—California—San Francisco. 2. Same-sex marriage—
United States. 3. Gay rights—California—San Francisco. 4. Gay rights—United
States. I. Title.
    HQ1034.U5K56 2014
    306.84'80973—dc23   2013010364

A British Cataloging-in-Publication record for this book is available from the
British Library.

Visit our website: http://rutgerspress.rutgers.edu

Manufactured in the United States of America

CONTENTS

ACKNOWLEDGMENTS

Without the insight, guidance, and encouragement of my mentors at the University of California, Santa Barbara, I could not have turned a burgeoning sociological interest in the San Francisco same-sex weddings into the book you now hold. I thank Verta Taylor for her unwavering support of me and of this project. She was irreplaceable as an editor—and as a cheerleader—and I benefited enormously from her generous feedback. More than anyone else, Jennifer Earl made me the scholar I am today. I admire and learned from her impressive work ethic, integrity, humor, and commitment to mentoring, and even from her occasionally frustrating refusal to accept thanks for what she understands to be simply doing her job as a mentor. I thank Leila J. Rupp for her insightful analysis of my work, for the questions that helped me clarify my argument, and for her commitment to my scholarship. I also thank her for her behind-the-scenes consultations with Verta about this project, especially when they impinged on precious vacation time. Barbara Tomlinson modeled the thinking life, and I learned a great deal from her intentionality and the care she took in her thinking and writing. More than a few times, BT was able to articulate what didn't work in a piece, such that I not only knew how to fix it, but was motivated to do so. It is a rare talent to be able to inspire cheerfulness in the face of a major revision. BT was also a supportive presence for the inevitable, discouraging moments I faced during this project, helping me identify what, *for my purposes*, did and did not matter.

I thank my Rutgers editor, Peter Mickulas, for his enthusiastic commitment to this project and the academic editors of the Families in

Focus series, particularly Peggy Nelson and Rosanna Hertz, for their thoughtful reviews of earlier drafts. I am also much indebted to Jaye Cee Whitehead for her review of the initial manuscript. I drew heavily on her constructive critique in the final phases of completing this book. Her review represents the best of the peer review process that makes academic inquiry a collective endeavor.

Finally, this work would not have been possible without the phenomenal support of my colleagues in the Advancing New Standards in Reproductive Health (ANSIRH) program of the Bixby Center for Global Reproductive Health at the University of California, San Francisco. I am especially indebted to Tracy Weitz and Lori Freedman, who both offered encouragement, feedback, and steadfast belief in this project. It is a rare privilege to work with such a talented and committed group of scholars. I owe a debt of gratitude to all of my fellow ANSIRHites for making it such a wonderful place to work.

Throughout this project and my academic career broadly, my family—both immediate and extended, blood and chosen—has provided diversions, laughter, perspective, and love. I cannot thank them enough, especially David, Barbara, Rebecca, and Susie Kimport, Bob and the late Helen Buggert, and Richard Buggert. Last, my love and appreciation to Matthew Villeneuve and our daughter, Mathilde, for the joy they bring to my life.

QUEERING MARRIAGE

CHAPTER 1

THE WINTER OF LOVE

*This really was our generation's Stonewall. It was an absolutely
unprecedented, thrilling, amazing, overwhelming experience. . . . It
just was this moment of love. That's why they call it 'the winter of
love' because it was a spontaneous outpouring of joy and love. And
the whole city was just bubbly.*

—Marriage equality activist

Gavin Newsom was sworn in as the mayor of San Francisco in January
2004. It had not been an easy climb to the top. Mayor Newsom entered
office following a highly contested political campaign during which he
found few allies in San Francisco's lesbian and gay community. Nonetheless, newly elected, young, handsome, married to an equally attractive
woman, and charismatic, Newsom showed political promise. Among
his first actions as mayor, he attended President George W. Bush's State
of the Union address and heard Bush's call for using constitutional
processes to restrict marriage to different-sex couples.[1] This troubled
Newsom. Although the gay and lesbian community had not played a
large role in his election, he recognized same-sex couples as members
of his constituency and perceived their exclusion from marriage as
discriminatory—and he had an idea how to fix it.[2]

When he returned to San Francisco, Newsom reached out to lesbian and gay rights activists about his burgeoning idea, asking them
whether they thought it would be helpful to the community. After a
few meetings and the encouragement of representatives from three
activist organizations, on February twelfth, around noon, Mayor
Newsom made history by directing city hall to issue marriage licenses
to same-sex couples in San Francisco.

No one involved in the whirlwind planning expected that more
than a handful of licenses would be issued before a court intervened

to stop the license-granting, so the mayor chose the recipients of those first licenses carefully. First up were Del Martin and Phyllis Lyon, icons of the lesbian and gay rights movement and partners for fifty years. Martin and Lyon married in a semi-private ceremony in a city hall office, with a dozen or so public officials, lesbian and gay rights activists, and members of the press in attendance. Soon after, city hall opened its doors to any couple who wanted to get married. So began what many participants called "the winter of love."

The timing of these events owed, in part, to Newsom's desire to bring his idea to fruition as quickly as possible, but it was also strategic. Beginning in the late 1990s, advocates for same-sex marriage designated February twelfth as "Freedom to Marry Day." Same-sex couples marked the occasion by traveling to their local city hall and requesting marriage licenses, making visible their exclusion from this cultural rite of passage. In 2004, as Martin and Lyon discretely married inside city hall, gay and lesbian couples gathered outside city hall with plans to request marriage licenses. Among them was Keith, a forty-five-year-old lawyer who had been committed to his partner, Tim, a forty-three-year-old policy analyst, for seventeen years. (Keith and Tim, as well as the names of all respondents discussed in this book, are pseudonyms.)

The year prior, as Keith and Tim sat down to complete their tax returns, they were frustrated yet again that each had to check the "single" box. It felt like a lie to represent themselves as unmarried after over a decade and a half of commitment. On top of that, they knew filing jointly would give them significant tax advantages. After mulling this over for several months, the two decided to become active in advocating for marriage equality. A more personal reason also motivated them: Tim's parents are an interracial couple, and Tim grew up acutely aware that the law for much of the twentieth century would not have permitted his parents to marry.[3] He knew what marriage meant to his parents and his family, and he saw that the law can change.

Despite their hopes that this would be the year they received a marriage license, Keith and Tim assumed they would be denied licenses. Along with the other couples lined up outside city hall, they intended to use the rejection as an opportunity to protest their exclusion from marriage. Some in the crowd had heard rumors that this year would be different, but no one knew for sure. In the short time that Newsom's plan came together, only an inner circle of activists were in the know. But this year *was* different: same-sex couples received the licenses they came to request. Almost immediately, a line of eager couples formed as the would-be protesters became newlyweds.

There were other, largely unanticipated, strategic advantages to the February twelfth date. The courts were closed that day for Lincoln's birthday. As expected, opponents of same-sex marriage quickly mobilized a petition to the state courts to cease the marriages, but no action could be taken that day. When the courts opened the next day, they declined to halt the marriages, allowing Lynn and Anne, together eleven years, to marry. As Lynn, a forty-six-year-old director of a senior center, remembered, it was "lucky Friday the thirteenth." That morning, while Lynn got ready in the bathroom, Anne, a fifty-four-year-old artist, poured herself a cup of coffee and read the headlines in the newspaper. She shouted to Lynn that same-sex weddings were happening at city hall. Lynn responded, "Do you want to go?" Anne replied, "Yeah, let's go!" Anne left her cup of coffee half-finished on the kitchen table and the two raced to city hall. As they recounted to me later, both were surprised at how much marriage mattered to them and, indeed, how much it changed their relationship.

City hall stayed open late that Friday, with staff members working overtime without pay to marry the couples lined up for licenses. It opened again on Saturday, Sunday, and Monday, despite Monday being President's Day and officially a government holiday. Isabel and Raine celebrated six years of commitment by marrying on Sunday, February fifteenth. Both grew up in cultures that heavily stressed marriage, and they wanted to honor their relationship by marrying. The two were also jointly raising the children each brought from a prior (different-sex) marriage. Isabel, a thirty-nine-year-old professor, in particular, felt that marriage would change how they all related as a family. They selected the day strategically. Raine, a forty-five-year-old retiree, is in a wheelchair, and waiting in line would quickly exhaust her. They had, Raine said, one shot. Together, they decided Valentine's Day would likely be too popular and hoped the following day would be less congested. Early in their wait, a volunteer told them they had a 1 percent chance of marrying that day, given the number of couples already ahead of them. They took that chance and several hours later received their license.

By the time the courts were back in session on Tuesday, hundreds of couples had married. Again, the courts declined to halt the marriages, and city hall continued to issue licenses through the end of the week. The line of eager couples snaked up and down hallways within city hall and then continued around the block outside. With city hall open late and over the weekend and newly deputized officials on hand, San Francisco was able to process a higher than average number of licenses in that time. Even then, they could not keep up with the demand. Barbara and Gayle, together three years, came back two days in a row to wait in line—despite Barbara's belief that marriage is a bourgeois institution that perpetuates inequality. Even as Barbara, a forty-eight-year-old electrician, remained suspicious of marriage, she could not help but acknowledge the pleasure she felt in being part of what she saw as an act of civil disobedience by thousands of gay and lesbian couples. At the end of the first full week of granting marriage licenses to same-sex couples, city hall switched to an appointment-only procedure. Soon there was a three-month wait for an open appointment. For these individuals, something significant was at stake.

What was not at stake was these couples' commitment to each other. For all intents and purposes, many considered themselves already married, using the term in the cultural sense to convey long-term commitment. And yet, notwithstanding their long-existing commitments to each other, these couples dropped everything to get to city hall. Anne and Lynn left their coffee half consumed at the kitchen table; Philip, a thirty-four-year-old project coordinator just starting a new job at a retail company, walked out of a morning meeting after receiving a text message that the licenses were being issued; and Phoebe, a thirty-seven-year-old analyst, drove overnight from Southern California with her partner, Alex, to get married. Gays and lesbians from throughout the United States and around the world came to San Francisco to marry, braving rain and bad weather, camping out overnight, and enduring hours and sometimes, like Barbara and Gayle, even days of waiting in line.

On March 11, 2004, four weeks after Mayor Newsom's executive order, the Supreme Court of California issued a stay, pending review of the case, ending the granting of marriage licenses. By that time, 4,037 same-sex couples representing forty-six states and eight foreign countries had received marriage licenses, and 3,955 of them managed to marry and get their marriages officially recorded. The San Francisco events were not the first instance of gay and lesbian activists agitating for the right to legally marry, nor were they the first public occurrence of same-sex weddings, but these events garnered extensive media coverage, in both the mainstream and gay presses, and captured the attention of the nation.

Controversy surrounded the mayor's decision at a national level, but in San Francisco, the events were joyous and celebratory. Lynn remembers watching Anne be overcome by emotion as the magnitude of the events dawned on her. Keith summed up city hall as "the happiest place on earth." An outpouring of goodwill welcomed lesbian and gay couples into the institution of marriage: cabs offered free rides to newlyweds, flower shops distributed free bouquets to those waiting in line, and bakeries offered slices of wedding cake to couples exiting city hall with their marriage licenses. People in and around city hall applauded, cheered, and cried tears of happiness. Volunteers lined up to be deputized to perform marriage ceremonies. Ernesto, a fifty-eight-year-old health educator, married Tony, his partner of twenty-eight years, the morning of the thirteenth and then, caught up in the excitement of the events, returned the next three days to volunteer at city hall, escorting couples through the process, managing lines, and acting as a witness. For the couples, their loved ones, and their allies, this was the Winter of Love.

Six months after the first same-sex marriage license was issued to Martin and Lyon, on August 12, 2004, the California Supreme Court handed down its unanimous decision that Mayor Newsom had exceeded his authority in issuing the licenses, although they declined to rule on the constitutionality of same-sex marriage more generally, effectively inviting future challenges to state marriage law. The court further ruled, three to two, to void all of the same-sex licenses. For the couples who had waited in line and paid their license fee, their certificate was now legally nothing more than a piece of paper. But although those newly minted licenses were no longer legally meaningful, the story of same-sex marriage was far from over. In fact, it was just the beginning.

In this book, through the stories that participants in the Winter of Love shared with me, I offer an up-close portrait of the weddings that helped galvanize a national movement for marriage equality. I empirically examine what happens when same-sex couples wed, what it means to them, and how it impacts their lives. This investigation, even as it foregrounds the personal experiences of gays and lesbians who married, situates their stories in the broader social meanings of marriage. Indeed, their offered meanings and reported impacts of marriage are always tacitly in conversation with contemporary ideas about marriage and provide a window into the institution itself. This book is an account of what the practice of same-sex marriage can tell us about society.

From the outset, it is important to remember that these weddings were only briefly legal; the California Supreme Court voided the licenses. And, as the accounts of some of my respondents detail, many participants never expected the marriages to last. Yet their narratives of the impact of those months of marriage on their lives belie the licenses' short-lived legality. It is worth emphasizing this point. In the stories shared in subsequent chapters, the immediate effect of the institution of marriage on respondents' lives *even though* their marriages were invalidated is clear; there is a qualitative effect of being married that is not dependent on the length of time couples were married.[4] Even as the legitimacy of the weddings was always precarious, these marriages *felt* real. That this feeling of authenticity overrode their rational assessments that the marriages would not last speaks to the utility of this case for exploring what happens when same-sex couples marry. It turns out that marriage has power even in brief doses. In the 2004 San Francisco wedding events, we have a defined group of couples who married within weeks of one another, in circumstances that drew the attention of the world. They were the first large group of same-sex couples to marry and they knew it. Their awareness made them keenly attuned to how and when marriage mattered in their everyday lives. In essence, they were a test case for same-sex marriage, and they demonstrated a demand for marriage that became part of a nationwide movement.

In the years since the Winter of Love, marriage equality has enjoyed significant successes, with same-sex couples gaining the right to marry in several states, and more than a few setbacks, including the passage of constitutional amendments rewriting state constitutions to restrict marriage to different-sex couples in other states. Polls point to increasing support for same-sex marriage, particularly among young adults, even as opponents agitate for a national constitutional amendment against it. Throughout these political and cultural shifts, scholars and pundits have widely speculated about the meanings and impacts of same-sex marriage.

Like San Francisco's Summer of Love in 1967, the Winter of Love promised to demonstrate a peaceful, loving, alternative way of being in the world. It was a protest over discrimination against lesbian and gay couples, it was a valorization of romantic love as the foundation of families, and it was a challenge to the status quo. Like the 1969 riots outside the New York City Stonewall Inn that are popularly credited with touching off the gay liberation movement, the Winter of Love was a transformative event. The question is, transformative of what?

TRANSFORMING SOCIETY OR TRANSFORMING GAY AND LESBIAN COUPLES

Many are hopeful that same-sex marriage will transform the meaning of marriage and, with it, society by disrupting the dominance of heteronormativity. Society privileges heterosexuality. As sociologist Chrys Ingraham (1994, 204) cogently argues, heterosexuality is "the standard for legitimate and prescriptive sociosexual arrangements." Heterosexuality is the norm. We assume, until told otherwise, that people are heterosexual, that they are attracted to people of a different gender from themselves. Think of the scenario of a mixed-gender couple requesting a hotel room for a night. The hotel would give them a room with one bed. However, if the two people approaching the hotel desk were both men, it is hard to imagine they would be offered a room with just one bed. They would likely get a two-bed room. Perhaps those two men do not mind the extra bed, but the underlying message the two-bed room sends is that they are not perceived as a romantic couple—their relationship is presumed platonic. The members of the heterosexual couple, on the other hand, can move through life without having to explain themselves.

There are myriad less benign examples of the ways heterosexual couples are privileged. Marriage is one of them. Throughout US history, rules and regulations surrounding marriage have regulated sexuality (Cott 2000), instituting different-sex relationships as normative and socially rewarded. According to the General Accounting Office (2004), legal marital status carries with it 1,138 federal benefits, including expedited citizenship for spouses, access to a spouse's social security benefits and/or government pension, and the financial advantages of filing joint tax returns. The exclusion of gay and lesbian couples from state-sanctioned marriage is a legal means by which the state endorses and rewards heterosexuality, since the rights and benefits of marriage are unavailable to the unmarried. The privileging of these particular relationships and their simultaneous marking as simply ordinary reinforces presumptions that everyone is heterosexual and, moreover, the prescription that heterosexuality is normal. In other words, they institute heteronormativity.

As a society, our unquestioned presumption of heterosexuality conceals this operation of heteronormativity. When heterosexuality is naturalized, its discursive production is concealed. Instead of recognizing the ways that law, culture, and language, for instance, privilege and reward heterosexuality, thinking of heterosexuality as universal and natural renders the benefits that accrue to heterosexuals—and the punishment of nonheterosexuals—invisible or, even worse, normal. Ingraham (1994) calls this the "heterosexual imaginary." Hiding in the imaginary, heteronormativity does not require explanation or critique and its institutionalization of inequality is perpetuated. Without pointed consideration, this is the way the world works.

Weddings are among the practices most commonly marked as heterosexual. Ingraham (1999; 2003) has argued that the romantic discourse around weddings masks the operation of transnational capitalism in the increasingly expensive business of having a wedding, a process that remakes the meaning of weddings to deemphasize love, commitment, and family and instead reinforce heteronormative expectations. Other work demonstrates that weddings continue to valorize heterosexuality over all other sexual identities. For instance, Ramona Oswald's (2000) analysis of interviews with lesbian, gay, bisexual, and transgender people about their experiences attending heterosexual weddings finds that members of the gay and lesbian community consistently report feeling hidden during these events and that the value of their own relationships was being questioned. For many in the lesbian and gay community, weddings and marriage are culturally associated with heterosexuality and heterosexism and are experienced with feelings of exclusion.

With same-sex marriage, some see an opportunity to disrupt the relationship between marriage and heteronormativity and to transform society by undermining (a component of) heterosexual privilege. In this group, scholars argue that the very presence of same-sex couples in a heterosexually dominated institution will undermine heterosexuality's normative power. Feminist philosopher Cheshire Calhoun (2000), for example, argues that when lesbian and gay couples can marry, the presumption that straight couples are "better" will be undone. Such advocates for same-sex marriage anticipate that including gays and lesbians in marriage, while continuing to privilege marriage as an institution, will assert the morality of same-sex relationships and homosexuality broadly. They hope that this will then translate culturally into increased equality for nonheterosexuals.

Along this vein, most expansively, some of these advocates claim that same-sex marriage can lead to gay and lesbian equality (Calhoun 2000; Eskridge 1993; Wolfson 2004). Others have similarly contended that access to marriage will help integrate gays and lesbians into society and bring an end to their second-class citizenship (Josephson 2005; Rauch 2004; A. Sullivan 1997). In this logic, the presence of same-sex couples in marriage will codify gays' and lesbians' position as legitimate citizens and induce broader society to question and ultimately reject policies and practices that privilege heterosexuals, realizing that such privilege amounts to discrimination. Legal scholar William Eskridge (2002) pushes further, arguing that same-sex marriage can unmake gender roles entirely, upending heteronormativity on a larger scale.

More narrowly, other activists and scholars have asserted that the presence of gay and lesbian couples in marriage will transform marriage—but not necessarily society—away from its heterosexist meanings. Sociologist Mary Bernstein (2001), for instance, argues that lesbian and gay participation in marriage cannot fail to undermine the institution's hegemonic notions of the family. Positing that gay and lesbian couples are, by definition, outside of normative assumptions of married couples, Bernstein argues that when same-sex couples marry, it upsets—and transforms—the very definition of marriage as a place of heterosexual privilege. Other sources of heterosexual privilege may persist, but the power of marriage to institute inequality based on sexual identity will be undone.

For this group of scholars and advocates, same-sex marriage holds great promise for improving the lives of same-sex couples as well as lesbians and gays, coupled or not, more broadly. While they vary in how expansively or narrowly they anticipate marriage and society will be transformed, they share in common a construction of the heteronormative meaning of marriage as changeable. Same-sex marriage, they argue, will contest heterosexual privilege and make ours a more equal society.

There is another possible transformative outcome of same-sex marriage, one that is not so sunny for gay and lesbian couples: same-sex marriage may have an assimilating effect. Paula Ettelbrick (1992) is one early advocate for caution about the utopian possibilities of same-sex marriage. Rather than liberate gays and lesbians, Ettelbrick warns, marriage could create further constraints; the simple act of including lesbian and gay couples in the institution does not fundamentally realign heteronormative power. Like Ettelbrick, some queer community advocates argue that the hegemony of heterosexuality and associated inequality will be further entrenched with legal same-sex marriage (Bernstein and Taylor 2013b). Distinct from the host of conservative scholars and activists opposed to same-sex marriage and also to homosexuality, these scholars characterize same-sex marriage as an institution that will establish the dominance of a heterosexual norm even within the lives of lesbians and gay men.

Mariana Valverde (2006), for example, identifies the emergence of what she calls the "respectable same-sex couple" that shares much in common with its heterosexual counterpart. The respectable same-sex couple presents itself according to normative gender conventions (read: no men in dresses) and voices narratives of family and finances, bridging the gap between same-sex and different-sex couples with recourse to the common challenges couples of all compositions face. Missing from these couples is any clear reference to sex—they are respectable, hiding their non-normative sexual practices from a general audience. Valverde identifies this couple as increasingly legally and culturally prominent, offering a less queer vision for gays and lesbians to aspire to than the gay liberation movement offered a few decades ago. Amin Ghaziani (2011) goes further, suggesting that the emphasis on the similarities of gays and lesbians to heterosexuals, rather than the differences between the two groups, represents a "post-gay" politics.

Respectable same-sex couples may easily gain access to the benefits of the state, and the so-called good gays may receive social encouragement, but what of those who do not fit into these legitimate categories? As sociologist Susanna Walters (2001, 349) argues, "gay marriage might grant visibility and acceptance to gay marrieds, but it will not necessarily challenge homophobia (or the nuclear family) itself; indeed, it might simply demonize nonmarried gays as the 'bad gays' (uncivilized, promiscuous, irresponsible) while it reluctantly embraces the 'good gays,' who settle down and get married." Those in relationships close to the margins of legitimacy may be encouraged through social expectation to conform to normative standards such as marriage and those in relationships far from the margins of legitimacy may be rendered even less legitimate (Butler 2002; Ettelbrick 1992). And as marriage becomes embedded in the gay and lesbian community as a normative practice, we might expect a decrease in the flourishing of counter-heteronormative family formations such as those Judith Stacey (2004), Adam Green (2006), and Dana Berkowitz (2009) document, and maybe even Kath Weston's (1991) complex chosen families that redefine the meaning of kinship.

Following these speculations to their conclusion, Lisa Duggan (2003) has suggested that success in the campaign for same-sex marriage would institute "homonormativity," wherein, in return for access to social institutions like marriage, gay men and lesbians would mute the queer critique of heteronormativity. In effect, homonormativity would complement heteronormativity, enabling its continued ubiquity, and demobilize advocates for more radical social change. It would not simply fail to contest heteronormativity, it would reify it. Instead of transforming society, same-sex marriage may institute norms for lesbians and gays.

The arguments about the transformative impacts of same-sex marriage, both those optimistic about its social consequences for equality and those more pessimistic, share a central engagement with the heteronormative character of marriage. Given that marriage is an institution that perpetuates heterosexual privilege, they are asking whether same-sex marriage will contest or reify heteronormativity, leading, on the one hand, to the undoing of heteronormativity and, on the other, to its further entrenchment.

This debate has many participants and an extensive paper trail, but these arguments remain largely speculative. Most are premised on the simple presence or absence of same-sex marriage, rather than on a nuanced understanding of same-sex marriage as a practice. The empirical data presented here demonstrates that the impacts of same-sex marriage on heteronormativity are far more complex than anyone anticipated. I find that gay and lesbian couples use marriage to explicitly contest heteronormativity. But so, too, is there evidence that participation in marriage changes same-sex couples in ways that suggest the shoring up of heteronormativity. The interesting part of the story—and what I focus on in this book—is how the practice of same-sex marriage can illustrate the stubbornness and tenacious appeal of heteronormativity in contemporary society.

The Ever-Changing Institution of Marriage

There is no intrinsic (heteronormative) meaning for marriage. References to "traditional marriage" aside, marriage is actually an adaptable institution whose meaning has changed significantly over time (Coontz 2005). Historically, marriage had the function of binding individuals into social groups and was used to control property and reproduction. Through marriage, the state carried out racist policies, including the denial of marriage to slaves and the prohibition of interracial marriage. These restrictions enabled white men to have sexual access to slave women and pathologized both black male and black female sexuality (Collins 2005). Similarly, through marriage, the state has enforced religiously inflected values of dyadic marital monogamy, as when the federal government demanded that Utah formally denounce the practice of polygamy before it was admitted to the union (Cott 2000).

With changes in the economy following the Industrial Revolution, new philosophical and political ideals, and increasing mobility, the social purpose of marriage changed from binding groups together. By the beginning of the twentieth century, marriage was increasingly understood to be best predicated on love. Ernest Burgess and Harvey Locke (1945) describe this evolution in the meaning of marriage as a transition from institutionally focused to what they term companionate marriage, where the emphasis is on compatibility and the functioning of the couple. Contemporary scholars have argued for a second, more recent transition in marriage's social function from companionate to individualized marriage (Cherlin 2004). In individualized marriage, the institutional aspect of the union has decreasing significance, following a general pattern of the weakening of social norms across the social world. Couples no longer marry primarily to please their extended families or for financially strategic reasons. Nor are children a universally motivating incentive for marrying and staying married (Giddens 1991). In individualized marriage, these social norms are replaced by an emphasis on personal choice and self-development wherein weddings and marriage become status symbols.

The decreasing institutional significance of marriage is evident not just in culture but also in law. The shifting focus on the individual has accompanied increased access to divorce and the removal of restrictions on interracial marriage, weakening marriage's institutional role in policing race and enforcing lifelong monogamy. Moreover, married status is no longer required to access many of the rights individuals accrue—marriage does not organize people's lives in the same way it has historically (Coontz 2005).

Throughout these changes in the institution, its overarching meaning as a heterosexual practice has not undergone significant revision. And yet, there are hints that the heterosexual underpinnings of marriage, just like other meanings of marriage, are not set in stone. Andrew Cherlin (2004) argues that some of the recent shift in the meaning of marriage toward a focus on the individual has rendered the restriction of marriage to different-sex couples unnecessary: procreation is not integral to a marriage and marriage is expected to provide individualized rewards, not social goods. We see evidence for this argument in the increasing numbers of gay and lesbian couples who are entering legal partnership recognition relationships. More than eighty-five thousand same-sex couples in the United States entered a legal relationship in the decade following 1997 (Gates et al. 2008). In states that allow the formal recognition of same-sex relationships through same-sex marriage, civil unions, or other forms of partnership, more than 40 percent of resident same-sex couples have completed such legal registration (Gates et al. 2008). These numbers, of course, have grown as additional states have legalized same-sex marriage.[5]

The participation of gays and lesbians in marriage represents a new opportunity to engage with marriage's meaning as a heterosexual practice and, potentially, to contest heteronormativity. As same-sex couples enter marriage, the question of how they navigate this meaning—and the privileges associated with it—is an open one. Will they eschew or embrace the heteronormative meanings of the institution? What happens when nonheterosexuals participate in a heterosexual practice?

ASKING QUESTIONS ABOUT THE MEANING OF MARRIAGE

Thanks in large part to the dearth of opportunities for same-sex couples to participate in marriage, we have little empirical evidence of what marriage means to gays and lesbians. Scholars who study same-sex marriage have offered various reasons for same-sex marriage—from legal rights to love to equality—but few have empirically analyzed how same-sex couples navigate marriage and its social meanings.

To think through the relationship between same-sex marriage and heteronormativity, we must look at the stories gays and lesbians tell about their marriages. We must ask Keith and Tim, who were among the first to marry on February twelfth, Anne and Lynn, who left their coffee unfinished as they rushed to marry on lucky Friday the thirteenth, and Isabel and Raine, who hoped marriage would bring them and their children together as a family, about their experiences. As sociological phenomena, couched in specific social context, narratives can secure or transgress dominant culture (Plummer 1995). With participants' stories about their marriages, we have the opportunity to analyze when and how same-sex marriage reifies or contests the heteronormative meanings of marriage as well as how participants navigate these meanings. In other words, we can better understand what the practice of same-sex marriage tells us about heteronormativity. In the end, the personal narratives of same-sex marriage give depth to our sociological understanding of the issue.

Among the few scholars who have traced the meanings of partnership recognition to same-sex couples in the United States, those offering the most extensive accounts have been limited to non-legal commitment ceremonies that did not take on the quality and character of legal marriage (for two excellent examples, see Hull 2006; Lewin 1998). Given the cultural and symbolic power of marriage—as a word and as an institution—however, analysis of commitment ceremonies rather than marriages *felt as legal* cannot tell us about the broader question of the impact of same-sex marriage on heteronormativity.

In the locales where same-sex marriage is available, scholars have pursued the question of its meaning to participants. After all, gay people are marrying, just not in much of the United States. These projects have analyzed the meaning of same-sex partnership recognition in the Netherlands (Badgett 2009), Denmark (Eskridge and Spedale 2006), Scandinavia (Rydstrom 2011), and the United Kingdom (Weeks et al. 2001). Each of these works engages important questions of the impacts of same-sex marriage, but there are limitations in the application of these findings to the United States. The history of the institution of marriage in each country is different, as is the social status of gays and lesbians, and the meaning of marriage varies by culture, underscoring the importance of attending to the specifics of the case of same-sex marriage in the United States.

In this book, I use stories of same-sex couples' experience of marriage during the San Francisco weddings to investigate how and when the practice of same-sex marriage reifies or disrupts marriage's meaning as a heterosexual practice. I take these events as an opportunity to empirically examine the meanings of marriage to same-sex couples who, thanks to these rare circumstances, were able to experience legal marriage, albeit briefly. With their stories, we can assess the (changing) relationship of marriage and heteronormativity.

Theoretical Framework

This book conceptualizes heteronormativity as an organizing social structure that produces specific behaviors and identities. Quite obviously, heteronormativity valorizes heterosexuality and initiates the social expectation that everyone is heterosexual. But it does still more.

As scholars of critical heterosexuality studies contend (see Ingraham 2005b), heteronormativity produces the simultaneous expectation that gender is oppositional and monolithic—you are either a man or a woman, attracted to your "opposite." There can be no gender without heterosexuality, nor can there be heterosexuality without gender. In this way, heteronormativity regulates both sexual (that is, sexuality) and social (that is, gender) identities (Ingraham 2005a), organizing not just sexual behavior but also the gender division of labor, distribution of resources, and patriarchal relations of production (Yep 2003). Simply put, heterosexuality is not just about sex, but about the social construction of behavior.

As a socially constructed structure, heteronormativity does not predate social relations: it exists through them. In interactions that take heterosexuality as universal and natural, heteronormativity is produced and reproduced. I use social theorist Pierre Bourdieu's (1977) theory of *practice* to understand the operation and reification of heteronormativity. Bourdieu posits that social structures determine practice: heteronormativity governs how the institution of marriage operates. As histories of marriage make clear, marriage has operated to structure gender and sexual relations in ways that normalize heterosexuality, both within and outside of the family (Cott 2000). This is not the end of the story, however. The relationship between social structures and practice is not as simple as structures determining practice: practice is also constitutive of social structures.[6] Structures like heteronormativity depend on constant reification for their authority. Without that reification, they lose their determinative power. To persist as a social structure, heteronormativity must be constituted by constant practice that takes heterosexuality as normal and natural.

In other words, the existence of social structures like heteronormativity is not a given, it is an ongoing production. Heterosexuality is not universal or necessarily central to society, but it is socially constructed as such through everyday practice (for two engaging examinations of this production, see Martin 2009; Martin and Kazyak 2009). In this book, I position marriage as one means through which heteronormativity is instituted—and quite successfully to date. But it does not have to be this way. Marriage is not inherently heteronormative, even if the practice of marriage historically has been. The history of a practice is not necessarily its future. Even as practice is partially determined by social structures, it also constitutes them, leaving room for resistance and resignification. It is that space this book is interested in. Participation in institutions like marriage can reify or, potentially, disrupt heteronormativity. Here I examine the relationship between the practice of same-sex marriage—a practice many have invested with the possibility of contesting heteronormativity—and heteronormativity, considering how practice is both determined by and constitutes social structure. In other words, this book investigates whether the practice of marriage by gay and lesbian couples will be largely determined by the overarching social structure of heteronormativity or will constitute the meaning of marriage differently (that is, not as a heterosexual practice) and contest heteronormativity.

Telling the Story of Same-Sex Marriage

In the following chapters, I draw on interview data from men and women who married in the 2004 San Francisco weddings to examine the meanings of marriage to same-sex couples and analyze the (changing) relationship between marriage and heteronormativity. I rely on three data sources: interviews with forty-two participants in the weddings; interviews with seven key informants, including public officials and activists representing the key marriage equality social movement organizations active in the Bay Area around the time of the weddings; and the March 2004 report from the San Francisco Assessor-Recorder's Office, which contains comprehensive demographic data on the gender, geography, age, and education of the men and women who applied for marriage licenses. Both sets of interviews were conducted in 2006. Together, these data sources allow me to offer descriptive depth on general patterns and meanings among the couples who wed in San Francisco in an effort to better understand their experience of marriage.

The forty-two participants interviewed represent sixteen lesbian and eleven gay couples. Fifteen couples were interviewed jointly and twelve respondents were interviewed on their own. Of the twelve cases where I was able to interview only one member of the couple, two instances were because the couple was no longer together (or, in the words of my respondents, they were "divorced"), one was because the respondent's partner had passed away, four were because the couple had young children and one member of the couple needed to be responsible for child care, three were because of scheduling difficulties, and, in the remaining two cases, the non-interviewed partner was not interested in participating for undisclosed reasons. Although the majority of my respondents were white, twelve of the twenty-seven couples were interracial. Generally, respondents were well-educated and had high incomes. They ranged in age from twenty-seven to sixty-eight and, at the time of their marriages, had been committed to their partner anywhere from a year and a half to fifty years, with an average of ten years together before the weddings. More detail on my data and research methods as well as comparison of my sample to the overall population of couples married is available in the methodological appendix.

There is no simple answer to the question of what same-sex marriage means to heteronormativity, but through the analysis of the stories and the storytellers we gain purchase over how and when this practice embraces and contests heteronormativity.[7] In chapters 2, 3, and 4, I examine three sets of meanings for marriage offered by respondents for how they navigate the institution's heteronormative character and what they suggest for the continuing hegemony of heterosexuality. In chapter 2, I discuss how participants actively mobilized marriage as a way to expose and contest heteronormativity, characterizing marriage as something political. In chapter 3, I investigate the apparently paradoxical embrace—voiced by many of these same participants—of the normative benefits of marriage, including its legal protections and the social legitimacy it confers. I show how some same-sex couples aim to only partially unmake marriage as a heterosexual practice, still preserving the privileges it affords for themselves. Next, in chapter 4, I examine framings for marriage that rest on the insistence that same-sex couples are just like straight couples. These meanings were offered by the fewest respondents, but are often found in public campaigns for same-sex marriage. I argue that, in focusing on individualistic meanings for marriage, they effectively bypass the question of heteronormativity altogether and do little to challenge sexual identity–based marginalization.

In chapter 5, I delve into some of the patterns in the invocation of these meanings for marriage. I find that gender, parenthood status, and race matter for how respondents engaged with the heteronormative associations of marriage. Women were more likely to mount a political critique of marriage as a heteronormative institution; parents were more likely to embrace marriage's normative meanings; and white respondents were more likely than respondents of color to identify marriage as a path to social legitimacy. These patterns showcase variation in the appeal of heteronormativity.

Finally, in chapters 6 and 7, I consider what same-sex couples' experience of marriage illustrates about heteronormativity. Chapter 6 discusses how marrying changed gay men's and lesbians' social interactions and how legal same-sex marriage may usher in additional changes. Even when respondents did not seek the normative perks of marriage, they nonetheless experienced them, demonstrating the persistence of heteronormativity. In chapter 7, I analyze some of the ways marrying made heterosexual privilege visible, both to participants and, potentially, to others, tracing the extensive reach of heteronormativity.

It was my privilege to hear the deeply personal stories of those who married in San Francisco. In sharing them here, I aim to illuminate the meanings they ascribe to the institution and the impacts, both expected and unexpected, of this legal status on their lives. These stories are, of course, personal and unique to the men and women who imparted them to me. But taken together they offer an opportunity to think through what the practice of same-sex marriage means to the pervasiveness of heteronormativity.

CHAPTER 2

MARRYING FOR
THE MOVEMENT

When I asked Robert, a thirty-six-year-old physical therapist, what his marriage to Brian, his partner of eleven years, meant to him, he paused for a moment. He continued stroking their cat as it sat docilely in his lap, looked around the beautiful sunlit kitchen in the home he and Brian, a forty-year-old lawyer, shared, and offered this answer: "It's interesting when you think about marriage. Certainly, for most people, the idea of being married has no connection whatsoever with making a political statement. But for us, obviously, it's unavoidable, inescapable. You definitely are aware of that. It's civil disobedience— you're doing what society's been telling you you can't do." In Robert's nuanced comment, several themes emerge. Most prominent is his description of his marriage as a political act, despite contemporary understandings of marriage as a personal union based on love. Also embedded in Robert's answer is an implicit collective identity. Robert draws a distinction between "most people" and "us," where his "us" includes not only Brian and himself, but gay couples more broadly. And the different social position Robert's "us" finds itself in is, to him, an obviously marginalized one.

Robert was not alone in seeing these marriages as political acts. Two-thirds of the men and women I talked to cited a political meaning for their participation (N = 28; 67 percent), marking "the political" as an important place to start in thinking through the San Francisco weddings. Respondents characterized their marriages as acts of civil disobedience that challenged the assumption that marriage is reserved for different-sex couples. The marriages were an opportunity to show solidarity with one another, make same-sex couples—especially "normal"-looking same-sex couples—visible, and build on the gains made by lesbian and gay activists who came before. Marrying, in other words, was an act that contested sexual identity–based inequality and discrimination; it was a challenge of heteronormativity.

Since the middle of the last century, activists have opposed the marginalization of lesbians and gays on several fronts, in an increasingly coherent movement (Fetner 2008). The movement has protested laws prohibiting public expressions of homosexuality and openly gay and lesbian teachers and policies preventing gays and lesbians from serving in the military and has advocated for policies that would benefit lesbians and gays, including employment nondiscrimination protection for sexual identity and quicker access to drugs used to treat HIV/ AIDS (Epstein 1996). It has contested homophobic attitudes through events designed to make lesbian and gay people visible (for example, kiss-ins, marches, drag performances) (Ghaziani 2008; Rupp and Taylor 2003). Through challenges to law and culture, the lesbian and gay rights movement has actively sought to draw attention to and dismantle heterosexual privilege. Their claims have ranged from ambitious (undoing heteronormativity all together; Armstrong 2002) to modest (including gays and lesbians because they are similar to straights; Bernstein 1997), but all have sought to change this group's social position.

To a small degree, the movement has used marriage to contest heteronormativity. As detailed below, a handful of same-sex couples have protested their exclusion from legal marriage over the years, but these protests never caught on in the broader movement. This changed with the San Francisco weddings. They were bigger and more popular than any prior same-sex marriage event. Indeed, San Francisco had to turn people away. The San Francisco marriages earned their place in history for being at the right time, in the right place. These people, in this place, were ready to do something to contest heteronormativity and make same-sex couples visible.

Campaigning for Same-Sex Marriage

The first reported court challenge to the exclusion of same-sex couples from state-sanctioned marriage was *Baker v. Nelson* (191 N.W.2d

185 [Minn. 1971], appeal dismissed, 409 US 810 [1972]). In May 1970, Richard Baker and Michael McConnell attempted to obtain a marriage license from Gerald Nelson, a Minneapolis clerk. Nelson denied their request and Baker and McConnell filed a lawsuit, claiming the refusal violated their rights. The case was eventually appealed to the Minnesota Supreme Court, which ruled against Baker in 1971. Lest the political motivations of Baker and McConnell be overlooked for a more romantic notion of marriage, McConnell stated of their appeal, "We want to cause a re-examination and re-evaluation of the institution of marriage. We feel we can be the catalyst for that. Our getting married would be a political act with political implications" (Star 1971).

Baker and McConnell lost their case, but the ruling did not stop same-sex couples from seeking marriage. Throughout the 1970s, at different marriage counters around the country, gay and lesbian couples sporadically requested marriage licenses. Sometimes, a sympathetic clerk granted the license, but the requests never led to systematic policy change. When couples were refused, they took their claims to court and repeatedly lost (for a full list of cases, see Kotulski 2004, 90).

The lack of favorable rulings in these cases did not fully assuage opponents of same-sex marriage, however. In 1975, Arizona became the first state to enact a Defense of Marriage Act (DOMA), explicitly defining marriage as between one man and one woman. Few states immediately followed Arizona's lead at the time, but the pace of DOMA adoption accelerated during the beginning of the twenty-first century, and most states in the nation now contain some form of DOMA on their books.

Then, in the early 1990s, legal contention over access to same-sex marriage began heating up with *Baehr v. Miike* (No. 91–1394 [Haw. Cir. Ct. 1st 1996]) in Hawaii. In 1993, the Hawaii Supreme Court ruled that the denial of marriage licenses to same-sex couples violated the state constitution's equal rights amendment, but it fell short of mandating same-sex marriage. Instead, the court remanded the case to the trial court for the state to show a compelling interest in restricting marriage to different-sex couples. Three years later, in 1996, Circuit Court Judge Kevin Change ruled that Hawaii had failed to demonstrate a compelling interest in limiting marriage to different-sex couples and ordered the state to begin issuing licenses to same-sex couples. This ruling, however, was stayed, pending appeal.

While *Baehr* galvanized many marriage equality supporters as well as opponents, in this instance, its opponents carried the day. In 1998, Hawaii passed the first state constitutional amendment, one-upping simple Defense of Marriage Acts with an addition to the state constitution that prohibited recognition of same-sex marriage. Hawaii was not alone. Alaska also passed a defense of marriage constitutional amendment at the time, and Nebraska and Nevada soon followed.

The behavior of states where contention was not immediately present, such as Arizona in 1975 and Alaska in 1998, underscores a constant theme in contention over same-sex marriage: the interplay between states. Because marriage is a state-granted right, both supporters and opponents of same-sex marriage alike have been highly attuned to judicial rulings and legislative decisions in states throughout the nation. Victories for marriage equality in some states have been countered with further entrenchment of restrictions in other states.

In 1996, the federal government weighed in on the issue. Although states grant marriage licenses, the federal government allocates numerous benefits based on the marital relationship (General Accounting Office 2004). Moreover, in order to manage the patchwork of marriage and divorce laws across the country, federal law stipulates that states recognize marriages and divorces performed in other states. As same-sex marriage gained traction in the Hawaiian courts, opponents in other states grew nervous. They feared not only that their state might be next, but also that they might be forced to recognize these marriages, and so proactively worked to prevent such an occurrence through DOMAs or constitutional amendments. The 1996 federal Defense of Marriage Act, passed by Congress and signed by President Bill Clinton, put those fears to rest. The federal DOMA established a federal definition of marriage as a legal union between one woman and one man and removed the requirement that states recognize same-sex marriages performed in other states (although states were still required to recognize other sorts of marriages performed in other states). This meant that, even if a same-sex couple were able to marry in one state, the rights and benefits associated with marriage would not automatically extend to other states.

Supporters of marriage equality continued to push forward in the courts, with the next significant legal victory, and then legislative compromise, occurring in Vermont. Following a 1999 Vermont Supreme Court decision in *Baker v. Vermont* (744 A.2d 864 [Vt. 1999]), holding that denial of marriage licenses to same-sex couples violated the Common Benefits Clause of the state constitution, the state was tasked with either offering marriage to same-sex couples or creating an alternative legal vehicle for giving the rights and benefits of marriage to same-sex couples. The Vermont legislature responded in 2000 by creating civil unions, a legal status available only to same-sex couples that carried all the rights and benefits of marriage at the state level without the label "marriage."

At the federal level, opponents of same-sex marriage introduced the Federal Marriage Amendment in Congress. The amendment stated that marriage can only take place between one man and one woman and that the US Constitution cannot be found to require the conferring of marriage status on any unions other than those between a man and a woman. The amendment got no traction in Congress but was endorsed by President Bush and other leading conservatives.

Undeterred by DOMAs, constitutional amendments, or the compromised status of civil unions, advocates of same-sex marriage pressed on and gained full-fledged success in Massachusetts in 2003. In November 2003, the Massachusetts Supreme Judicial Court ruled in *Goodridge v. Department of Public Health* (798 N.E.2d 941 [Mass. 2003]) that the denial of marriage licenses to same-sex couples violated the state constitution. It ordered the state to begin issuing licenses in 180 days. Based on the constitutional amendment process in Massachusetts, there was no way for the opposition to delay legal same-sex marriage in the state and, on May 18, 2004, Massachusetts began issuing marriage licenses to same-sex couples.

By the start of 2004, same-sex marriage had become a social, political, and personal issue not just in the United States but around the world. Legal marriage was imminent in Massachusetts. Around the globe, several countries had already legalized same-sex marriage, including the Netherlands in 2001 and Belgium and Canada (the provinces of British Columbia and Ontario) in 2003, and several other countries offered legal equivalents under different names (for example, Norway). Simultaneously, in opposition to same-sex marriage, by 2004, thirty-seven states had enacted DOMAs, often as a constitutional amendment and not simply a law, and the federal DOMA remained in effect.

Same-Sex Marriage in California

California has been at the forefront of marriage law throughout the last century. From legalizing interracial marriage in 1948 to being one of the first states to allow no-fault divorce, it has been among the first states to adopt changing marriage laws that subsequently became standard throughout the country. In examples like interracial marriage, change has been in the direction of expanding access to marriage. The state's history on same-sex marriage, however, is more checkered (for more detail than offered below, see Lofton and Haider-Markel 2007).

Until the early 1970s, California marriage law was gender neutral (Lahey and Alderson 2004). In 1977, California amended the family code to specify that marriage was to be exclusively "between a man and a woman." For nearly two decades, no further action was taken on the issue. In the 1990s, opponents of same-sex marriage moved to enact a formal DOMA in California. Led by Assemblyman Pete Knight, whose son had estranged himself from the family by coming out as gay and actively campaigning against homophobia, the California State Assembly passed a bill banning same-sex marriage in 1995. The state senate—California's other legislative body—however, failed to support the bill. The subsequent year, Knight again introduced the bill but ultimately withdrew it, believing he did not have enough votes to win passage.

As the state legislature moved to deny same-sex couples access to rights associated with marriage, gay and lesbian advocates were pushing a domestic partnership law guaranteeing benefits to gay and lesbian government employees' partners. Berkeley became the first city in the nation to extend employee benefits to unmarried couples of any gender in 1984 and San Francisco followed suit in 1989. In 1999, as Knight and his cohorts were brainstorming on how to prevent same-sex couples from marrying, the state legislature voted to establish a state-wide registry that granted hospital visitation and health benefits to domestic partners of state employees.

Stymied by the state legislature, Knight took his DOMA bill to California voters in the form of an initiative in November 2000. Proposition 22, also known as the Knight Initiative, was a fourteen-word act that defined marriage in California as exclusively between one man and one woman. Proposition 22 passed with 61 percent of the vote and became law.

However, the issue was not put to rest, and three years later the state legislature voted to expand domestic partnership benefits to include virtually all the rights and responsibilities of marriage. The change took effect on January 1, 2005. As of that date, domestic partners in California were, in legal terms, nearly equivalent to different-sex married couples. They were required, for example, to file joint tax returns with the state. The legal name of their union, however, was not "marriage."

Marriage as Protest

While courts and legislatures throughout the United States debated same-sex marriage, advocates for marriage rights for same-sex couples moved into the streets. As Amin Ghaziani (2008) artfully describes, the question of marriage rose to the center of discussion about the 1987 March on Washington for Gay Rights. In organizing meetings leading up to the march, a group named Couples, Inc. argued for the representation of not just individual gay and lesbian rights claims but also claims for couples' rights. Noting that lesbian and gay couples experience specific discrimination that differs from that single people experience (Chambers 2001), Couples, Inc. pushed for couples' rights to be included on the march's agenda. This push for inclusion was not without its detractors. Other organizers questioned whether the gay rights movement should support coupling, suggesting that such a move ran counter to a movement premised on sexual liberation.

In the end, they agreed to add a demonstration on behalf of couples' rights: a collective wedding. On October 10, 1987, several thousand lesbian and gay activists demonstrated in front of the Internal Revenue Service building in what became known as "The Wedding." In this overtly activist event, couples on the street symbolically married en masse. The event was designed to call attention to how exclusion from marriage led to the unequal treatment of same-sex couples—compared to different-sex couples—in tax policy (Ghaziani 2008).

The rise of commitment ceremonies in the latter decades of the twentieth century has similarly been cast as a political phenomenon, even absent political intent by the committing couples. Kathleen Hull (2006), for example, argues that lesbian and gay commitment ceremonies are inherently political. She argues that they are the enactment of a cultural ritual in the absence of legal sanction and thereby draw on the power of culture to speak back to the limits of the law. Likewise, though none of the couples in Ellen Lewin's study (1998) framed their events in explicitly political terms, some did use their ceremonies as sites of resistance. For instance, many of the couples borrowed and consciously remade the symbols of marriage, asserting the legitimacy of commitment between lesbians or gay men. This assertion, Lewin argues, is fundamentally political.

In the late 1990s, gay and lesbian rights activists consciously adopted marriage as a protest tactic. More precisely, they deployed the tactic of requesting a marriage license for a same-sex couple at county clerks' offices. On February 12, 1998, the Lambda Legal Defense Fund, an advocacy organization for gay and lesbian rights, sponsored the first annual Freedom to Marry Day. On this day, in San Francisco and Seattle, same-sex couples applied for marriage licenses. They were denied, but their act made visible their exclusion from marriage. Through annual usage, these requests became a protest tactic of the burgeoning marriage equality movement, but the movement still lacked a place on the national stage. The San Francisco weddings changed that.

Participant Activists

More than any other aspect of the San Francisco weddings, the people made it historic. The sheer volume of individuals who wanted to marry or support those who did distinguished these events from others that preceded them. But the couples who married were not just any old couples. Many of them were activists, and this activist background helped them recognize the significance of their participation and overcome the many discomforts—long lines, wet weather—their participation entailed. Their protest experience convinced them that their action was worth it.

Most of the participants I interviewed reported a high level of activism, or former activism, although rarely for marriage equality. As table 2.1 shows, most respondents characterized their participation in protest as very high at some point in the past, if not at the time of the 2004 weddings. Before the marriages, however, few engaged in protest on behalf of same-sex marriage. Of the seven respondents who mentioned some involvement in the campaign for same-sex marriage prior to 2004, only two described themselves as active on the issue, with the remaining five characterizing their involvement as minimal. Using survey data, Verta Taylor and colleagues (2009) make a similar argument, finding that the participants in the San Francisco weddings had a high level of prior involvement in social movements, in general, and the LGBT, AIDS, and women's movements, in specific. When Mayor Gavin Newsom opened the doors of city hall to same-sex couples to apply for marriage licenses, he extended this opportunity to a politicized community. And lesbians and gay men walked through those doors to make a political statement.

Like Robert, who opened this chapter, many of the couples who participated in the San Francisco weddings aimed to make political statements, plural. They recognized the San Francisco weddings as a unique and poignant opportunity to engage in advocacy on behalf of lesbian and gay rights.

For Keith, the lawyer, the initial desire to wed in San Francisco was about accessing the benefits of legal marriage. As we saw earlier, when Keith and Tim sat down to complete their tax returns for 2002, they were struck by how different their tax payments would be if they were allowed to marry: "because we had uneven amounts of income between the two of us, it turned out that we would pay that year around 50 percent more in taxes." If they could marry—and both would happily commit to legal marriage—their financial situation would improve. But, for Keith, thinking about same-sex marriage simply as a vehicle for accessing legal benefits was only the beginning. Keith felt forced to lie on those tax returns: after over a decade and a half of commitment, he and Tim still had to check the box on their tax forms that said "single." He explained, "It says, 'single, married.' And there was a moment that year, with our own hand, we were forced to, in a sense, lie, to sign under penalty of perjury that for then sixteen

TABLE 2.1

RESPONDENTS' PERSONAL HISTORIES OF ACTIVISM
PRIOR TO THEIR 2004 WEDDINGS

| | | Engagement in marriage equality activism | | |
		Active	Minimal	None
General level of activism	Very high	0	2	9
	High	1	1	5
	Low	1	1	8
	Formerly active	0	1	12
	None	—	—	1
	TOTAL	2	5	35

years together that we were single." Keith realized that the excess taxes he and Tim paid each year were going, as he said, "to a government that wouldn't recognize our basic rights and our rights as a family." It was no longer just about being able to marry and pay lower taxes. Marriage equality was about Keith and Tim, as gay men, being treated equally. Keith said that it was about their dignity as human beings.

Pierre and Dale's story illustrates how many participants construed their marriage as marriage for the movement. When Pierre, a forty-three-year-old project development director, and Dale, a forty-two-year-old night club manager, decided to celebrate three years of commitment by formally registering as domestic partners, they wanted to make the occasion special. They planned to wear tuxedos, with matching boutonnieres, and share champagne afterward with the two close friends they had invited to serve as their witnesses. But despite their interest in making the event memorable, neither Pierre nor Dale invested a great deal of time preparing for their domestic partnership registration—they scheduled the appointment to complete their paperwork for just two weeks after agreeing to take this legal step. Domestic partnership was important in their relationship, with personal benefits, but they did not ascribe any larger meaning to their intention. This was especially true because Pierre is not a US citizen; he is Canadian. He is able to legally reside in the country under a work visa. He and Dale knew that domestic partnership paperwork would not enable him to stay in the country should he lose his job. It was a symbolic act for the two of them.

This changed when Mayor Newsom invited same-sex couples to marry two days before Pierre and Dale's scheduled domestic partnership registration ceremony. Immediately, their act took on more significance to them both. Dale called Pierre and proposed marriage. Pierre accepted without a moment's hesitation, but his reason for saying "yes" to marriage was not the same as his reason for saying "yes" to the domestic partnership. While the domestic partnership was a personal step, marrying meant being part of something bigger: Pierre was participating in a movement. He explained, "I haven't done a great lot of protesting in my life, but I have always tried to stand up for what I believe in. In this case, it was a really big example of standing up for what I believe in, not just paying lip service to it but actually being a part of it. Going out there and being in front of all these people, being there in front of the news media. And I couldn't have been happier. It seemed like the right thing to do." Like Pierre, most respondents did not see their participation as occurring in a vacuum. Instead, they situated the weddings in a history of action on behalf of lesbian, gay, bisexual, and transgendered people. Referencing a collective queer identity, Pierre said, "[The weddings] seemed like the normal, natural next step, the progression of our rights coming into being." Pierre and others saw the weddings as part of a coordinated series of challenges to discrimination; the weddings were part of a movement.

Terrance, a fifty-three-year-old retiree, felt he participated more for the movement—and for others who could not—than for himself. He said, "You really got caught up in just how special it was. Here you are in a major city of the world and you're doing something that a lot of people will never have an opportunity to do. In essence, for those for whom the dream of marriage is so important, you're helping them with their dream. For you, it's like, oh my gosh, we're really doing this and isn't it great to be in a city and have a leader where you can have this opportunity. Definitely started getting really caught up in the excitement." Terrance and others connected their participation to a claim *for* marriage and a claim *against* the unequal treatment of lesbians and gays in society.

In early 2004, the movement's epicenter was the Winter of Love—it mattered that these weddings took place in San Francisco. As Terrance's comment suggests, the city was fantastically supportive of the weddings. Days into the weddings, as Marnie, a fifty-seven-year-old accountant, waited in line in the rain, she said, "People were coming by with coffee and doughnuts and warm socks and things. Everybody wanted to be in on it." Bakeries supplied free slices of wedding cake and flower shops handed out bouquets and boutonnieres to the couples in line. Often, support came in the form of smiles, waves, and honks from passers-by. As Diana and Mia waited their turn on the street outside city hall, Diana, a fifty-one-year-old administrative assistant, remembers, "There was a lot of wonderful support, great expressions from people who just wanted to say, 'Good for you' and 'It's about time. We support you,' even people who would honk and wave, who didn't know what to do." Couples experienced applause and cheers as they exited city hall, license in hand. Cabs displayed signs offering free rides to newlyweds and restaurants around the area offered free use of their bathrooms to people as they waited in line. In these simple—and joyous—experiences, we can see the support of the city.

And respondents appreciated the feeling of inclusion. The city hall staff, in particular, impressed respondents with their commitment to marrying as many couples as they could, while keeping a friendly attitude. Ernesto, the health educator, fondly remarked, "They were mostly donating their time. They were working for free. They were going to work through the weekend and after hours and whatever. And they just offered to work because they believed so much in this—they believed in it. [There was] always this natural gentleness and smiles and encouragement. There was nobody that acted crass or grumpy." Even after hours upon hours of work, the staff and volunteers kept their spirits up and made each couple's experience a special one. Raine, the disabled retiree, was amazed at their efforts:

> You could just see they were wiped, yet there was no less emotion from them and excitement for us at four o'clock in the afternoon than there was for the people that were at 8:00 a.m. three days earlier. I mean, these people were truly just beyond themselves excited

for what they were doing for us. It was amazing. And yet, you could just see, they looked like shit. I mean, they were wiped. But they were so excited for us and they'd still be crying and tears and they'd see these little families come in and stuff. And it was just, God, I just couldn't imagine: would I have given that much? It makes you question: how much would you really give? Those people, sure, they gave a lot.

Phoebe, too, was touched by their efforts after she drove overnight to reach city hall. Asked what most struck her about her wedding experience, she said, "I think it was how excited the folks that were working that day were. The people that were actually swearing people in to be marriage commissioners, the people that were coming in on their days off to work, to file paperwork, and to make sure everyone got their licenses taken care of. They had such care. The people that were there cared so much about making sure that this was a great day. It was almost like they were glad that they were allowing same-sex marriages that day. That was very, very nice." And it did not go unnoticed that most of these staffers and volunteers were straight. Indeed, much of the support seemed to come from heterosexuals. Raine remembered, "The most beautiful thing was a heterosexual couple that had been married—she's in her wedding gown and he was in his tuxedo—and they came back and they were handing out bubbles to everybody that was getting married. And that was really cool. There was a lot of that."

As the expressions of support mounted, claims by opponents were barely noticed. Interviewees mentioned seeing a handful of protesters carrying signs in opposition to same-sex marriage but not much else. For the most part, participants ignored the protesters and celebrated instead. Sonia, a fifty-three-year-old public employee, related, "There were people picketing and saying why we shouldn't be doing this and all that, but that was very much overshadowed by the support and just the joy and happiness that just kind of hung in the air. It was just all around us." As respondents told it, city hall was a fantastic place to be.

San Francisco was also a particularly apt site for these events for less positive circumstances. Keith, the lawyer, cited the city's history as the first to elect an openly gay city official, Harvey Milk, in 1977. Milk's tenure as a San Francisco supervisor was short-lived. Eleven months into his term, he and Mayor George Moscone were assassinated by former supervisor Dan White in what is commonly understood to be a sexual identity–motivated hate crime. Keith said, "Something that did not escape the attention of many of us is that this is the same building where Harvey Milk and George Moscone were assassinated. It's a building that reverberates with symbols of meaning to San Francisco. To be getting married in that building where he was assassinated gives it a sense of history, of movement, of time, of continuing movement, being part of a larger history." In this way, the Winter of Love was potent symbolically for its location. While city hall had once been the site of a homophobic hate crime, in the mass weddings it was a site where gay and lesbian couples were embraced.[1]

The Line

For those who married in the first days of the weddings, when applicants had to wait in lines that often stretched around the block, the line itself was a unique experience. Unlike other lines, this line was patient and noncompetitive. Brian, the lawyer, explained, "I would say overall it was that, it was not your typical—it was the opposite of your typical being-in-line experience. Whereas, when you're in line there's almost a somewhat adversarial feeling or you don't interact in a positive way, or at all, or it's neutral at best when you're in line at Disneyland or at the bank or wherever. It's cordial at best. This was just high energy where everyone was smiling at each other, talking to each other, cheering for each other, sharing their stories. It was like a giant family reunion. Just something very different and very, very unique." The line experience Brian's comment evokes is one of collectivity, illustrating the potent sense of shared identity among the participants.

The line experience was so powerful that Janet and Cynthia got caught up in the collective experience of the events and married without ever firmly deciding they would. Saturday morning, February fourteenth, they dressed up and drove from their South Bay home to San Francisco. They needed to go to the city to pick up theater tickets and figured they would stop by city hall to check out the weddings as long as they were already nearby. Wary of the length of the line, they took a place in it anyway, enjoying the atmosphere, just to see what would happen. Janet, a fifty-three-year-old nurse, described the excitement of being in line:

They had dogs with the families. They had kids and the kids were all out on the lawn, playing around, whatever. And people would go by and they were honking and they would get all excited. And somebody would come out with a certificate and everybody cheering and wow! People came along and gave out flowers that they had picked up at the flower mart. A girl came along with a Polaroid camera and took pictures of people that didn't have cameras with them. People came around and gave out the little Valentine's Day candy. They came around and gave out juice or something, something to drink.

Next thing they knew, they had been waiting for six hours.

Much of that time they spent waiting, Janet was sure Cynthia, a fifty-seven-year-old federal employee, would decide she had had enough. As Janet explained, Cynthia hates to wait in any line, even at the grocery store, and Janet felt sure that would be the deal breaker: "She just goes shopping and whatever. Then, 'here, you stand on line.' Even going to the airport! No matter where there's a line, it's like we get in line and she's gone. That's what I really thought was going to be our undoing. I figured by the time I went and got the cash and got her coffee and got back, I was afraid she was going to say, 'I've been on line long enough. We're leaving.'" But the camaraderie of the city hall line made it enjoyable to Cynthia. She explained that she asked Janet to run those errands expressly so she did not have to leave the line—"I was having so much fun on line." The time flew by. Janet said, "It was just a party kind of atmosphere. And everybody was standing on line and we were standing for hours and nobody really cared." Only near the end of their wait did it fully register in their minds that they were about to marry. Cynthia said, "We realized probably about two hours before we actually got married, hey, this is for real. So we actually called some friends up and said, 'Want to come down?'" Cynthia agreed to get married, in some ways, as an afterthought. Before, she never would have agreed to stand in line for six hours. After, she was glad she did.

Elizabeth and Laura marveled at the line for the opposite reason: for being part of it so briefly. Laura is in a wheelchair and waiting in line for hours would have been highly taxing. Soon after she and Elizabeth got in line on February twentieth, a staffer came by and invited them to skip to the front of the line. After their expedited line experience, Elizabeth, a fifty-four-year-old accounting assistant, was struck by the encouragement they received from the very people they had skipped over: "Folks that we had cut in front of were just really happy for us." The city hall line was a collective place, where men and women (gay and straight) stood together to express their desire for same-sex marriage, in the face of a law that denied it.

This collectivity was instrumental not just in contesting a heterosexual norm, but also in increasing solidarity among those outside that norm. Several interviewees reported that much of their experienced joy came from a feeling of solidarity and community. Philip, age thirty-four, for example, was emotionally touched not so much by his own wedding to Steven, but by being able to witness the marriages of others. He said, "It was just emotional seeing everyone, 'cause everyone had their own story. It was really interesting to see that. There were a lot of people that were very emotional. I think a lot of older couples had waited for this day to come, people that had been together for twenty, thirty years. That was really emotional for them. It was hard for me, personally, to see that. I can't imagine waiting that long to be happy about something. That was pretty emotional, seeing the older couples." Philip's account references the changing status of gays and lesbians in American society and implicitly cites the social movement organizing that has helped achieve this. Contextualizing the San Francisco events as an opportunity to build and express solidarity with one another was one way in which participants underscored the protest aspect of their weddings.

Collective Visibility and Solidarity

Participants registered their challenge to heteronormativity in more ways than by simply showing up. They disrupted the social presumption of heterosexuality by being seen. Through the San Francisco weddings, same-sex couples were visible on the national—and perhaps even global—stage, asserting the legitimacy of an alternative to the heteronormative ideal. They challenged both the hegemony of the different-sex couple norm and the presumption that homosexuality is unnatural.

Craig, a research manager, was among those most concerned with using the weddings to achieve this visibility. Age sixty at the time of the interview, Craig remembered the loneliness and difficulty of growing up without any gay role models. To the extent that the visibility afforded by the San Francisco same-sex marriages could combat those feelings of social isolation for others, Craig felt compelled to participate. He said, "Just being visible and out there is hugely important. Every young gay kid believes they're the only one. In my case, it was because I was from a really small town and the only gay person I knew was a really crazy woman who, periodically, would be hospitalized in a mental hospital for months at a time. So my view of a gay person was not positive and was scary. So that visibility was absolutely something that I wanted to do." Craig drew on his own experience as motivation for participating, hoping to show young boys like he once was that there are happy, committed gay couples in the world. He participated with an invisible audience in mind, aiming to show closeted lesbians and gays what it might mean for them to come out.

Other respondents similarly recognized the imperative of visibility but had a different audience in mind, demonstrating that identity can be deployed strategically for multiple audiences and goals (Bernstein 1997; Taylor and Whittier 1992). Diana, the administrative assistant, emphasized the way the weddings made lesbians and gays visible to a national, mainstream, and presumably predominantly heterosexual audience:

> There needs to be something every year that does that, so that we're out there and so that the world, and certainly the United States anyway, sees that the number of people who are gay grow[s]—not that they grow but people who are out [as gay] grows—[sees] that they've always been among you; they've always been part of your family; they've always been the ones that are the butt of your jokes. They're out there. They're strong people. They come from all over the United States—we had people from the Midwest coming in that were in the same line. Alaska, other countries came in. It was just an opportunity for the citizens of the United States to see that we're here and we're not going anywhere.

Referencing her own experiences and awareness of the general perception that lesbians and gay men are "uncommon," Diana saw the weddings as an opportunity to communicate the presence of gays and lesbians throughout the country.

Diana also discussed the power of the events to show the racial diversity of the community. Herself Asian American, in an interracial relationship with a white woman, Diana saw the weddings as a space to show America that gays and lesbians come in all colors. Addy, a thirty-one-year-old of Native American and white heritage, was similarly struck by the diversity of presentation at the weddings. Indeed, she became emotional thinking about it, saying, "A lot of times I felt like crying, because when I looked behind me or looked in front of me, there were all these families, mixtures of people, different cultures, different backgrounds. You're in city hall and you see all these different couples of all these different colors. That was pretty darn cool. You saw white people with black people. You saw Native American people with white people. You saw short, tall, everything." In Mary Bernstein's (1997) formulation, this sort of identity deployment qualifies as a form of education, challenging the dominant culture's perception of lesbians and gays. The people participating on this stage reminded the general population of the needs and wants of gays and lesbians. It was an opportunity to demand attention and thus an example of the strategic deployment of identity toward political goals.

Along these lines, some participants saw the weddings as an opportunity to re-sculpt what media attention lesbians and gays do receive. In contrast to stereotypes about both the appearance and behavior of gay men and women, participants perceived those wed in San Francisco as more mainstream. Several, like Kelly, a thirty-nine-year-old professor, explicitly noted their pleasure at the way the weddings made "normal" gays and lesbians more visible and opposed negative constructions of homosexuality. Kelly said, "I saw what we were doing as a form of political protest too because it was, you know, counter to all the hegemonic messages of society that say queer people are queer in the bad sense. So I thought that it was challenging all kinds of images about us." Kelly and others remarked on the importance of the images the weddings telegraphed to the world about lesbian and gay couples. These were images of happiness, joy, love, and commitment—images of normativity—rather than images suggesting promiscuity, cross-dressing, or sadomasochism.

Terrance, the retiree, shared a similar sentiment. He explained, "The political part for me was to be given an opportunity to even do this, to be counted, to be amongst the couples who got married and didn't do it in jock straps and were halfway nude or with dresses on if you are a guy and slacks on if you are a woman. By the way, there's nothing wrong with that, but that's just not the type of gay person I am." Terrance and others emphasized the importance of this kind of visibility. The weddings showcased a homosexuality that was happy, diverse, and relatively mainstream—a homosexuality that was not, in other words, deviant. His recognition that there were "good" images of gays and not-so-good images illustrates the awareness within this population that the world was watching and a desire to put its best foot forward. Even as these couples told of experiences of social marginalization because of their sexual identity, certain presentations were discouraged during the weddings. I found no evidence that this discouragement was explicit—no one reported being told to dress in a certain way. Nonetheless, patterns in representation emerged in the population, suggesting that at least some implicit regulation was operating during the events: there were no men in dresses (Klmport 2012).

Respondents reported that this was important. Cynthia explained, "It was a positive event and environment that showed gay relationships in a positive environment, not a negative stereotype. Usually you see drag queens out there." Her partner, Janet, echoed that idea: "There were normal-looking people." Perceiving these to be uncommon media images of same-sex sexuality, respondents were expressly pleased at the opportunity to participate in their creation.

Some respondents hoped that through these images and legal same-sex marriage, bridges could be built between gay and straight populations and the divisions between them ultimately undone. Tim, the policy analyst, for instance, argued that the weddings showed straight America that lesbians and gays were not only all around them, but deserving of *all* of the same rights, not just access to marriage: "I think that, in a sense, marriage itself is a tactic in that humanization. I think that if our straight brothers and sisters saw us as completely, equally human then all this other stuff would flow: well, of course you deserve the same healthcare; of course you deserve the same rights from one state to another; of course you deserve equal immigration rights; of course medical studies should study your risk areas equally— whatever the issue might be." Through increased visibility, Tim and others hoped, heteronormativity could be undone and equality across sexual identity could be achieved.

Personal Visibility

Other participants embraced the weddings as an opportunity to assert a different kind of visibility, remaking not just stereotypes of gays and lesbians but also assumptions about their own sexual identity. There is evidence in published accounts of same-sex marriage that lesbian and gay individuals consciously deploy the power of the marital institution to signify their identity (see, for example, Sherman 1992). Marriage forces others to read individuals through their partners, signaling them as lesbian or gay and rendering their sexual identity visible (Kimport 2012). Several respondents commented on the way in which marriage—the public association of themselves with their same-sex partner—was a way of being "out." Sonia, the public employee, used her marriage as an opportunity to make sure everyone knew she was gay: "I actually sent out an email. I felt like all those people in my life—I came out very late in life—and all those people who didn't know, weren't sure, thought maybe. I wanted to clarify. So I sent out an email [telling them I got married]." Just as many participants hoped the weddings would change assumptions about lesbians and gay men as a group, some individuals like Sonia used the marriages to change assumptions about their own sexual identity.

Similarly, Deirdre, a thirty-seven-year-old writer, passes as heterosexual (unintentionally) and so actively uses her partner—and her marriage—to signal her homosexuality. She explained, "I don't code typically. You wouldn't guess looking at me that I'm a lesbian, right? Most people assume I'm straight because most people assume you're straight unless you do something that's obviously coded as otherwise. My strategy is I just find a way to come out, usually within the first five minutes that I'm in a room, say 'my partner,' 'my wife,' mention my son: 'his other mom and I, blah, blah, blah.' I just get it out there." Marriage was a tool for some participants to challenge normative assumptions about their sexual identity. It operated at the level of personal relationships, disrupting presumptions of heterosexuality. For some, the weddings were a political act that signaled something about their person.

Taking the Risk

Although San Francisco was a physically safe space for gays and lesbians, their participation entailed other kinds of risk. Marriage might negatively impact couples in terms of their taxes (Alm et al. 2000) or welfare eligibility (Hunter 1995), and some worried that marriage would invalidate other legal protections, including legal contracts and domestic partnership registrations. Putting the goals of the group ahead of their own, respondents explained that they understood the risks they were taking. For example, Carrie, a thirty-seven-year-old social worker, acknowledged that there could be costs from her and Lois's participation, but they were willing to assume those costs for the purposes of making social change. She said, "There was this talk that maybe people's domestic partnerships would be threatened, what would happen with the mayor, and was the city going to get in trouble? [Nonetheless, we were] standing up in the face of that and saying this is the way that change happens. And just knowing, historically, that this is sometimes how change has to happen—I think that that was very powerful." The stakes were worth it. Jeffrey, a sixty-three-year-old retired physician, explained, "Every once in a while, you need to do something—and it's almost like, you know, in your face. Because you've got to, at some point, you've got to stand up."

Carrie and others assessed the risks of participating in the weddings through tacit comparison of the San Francisco weddings and the movement it represented to other movements for social change. It was from these movements that respondents drew their conviction that the risks they were taking were necessary and important. Diana, the administrative assistant, for example, cited her participation as part of a larger, progressive series of movements: "It's like women's right to vote. It's like the civil rights movement. We are the next of those. We are the ones—first it was women's right to vote, then it was civil rights, now it's gay rights." Identifying a decades-long progression toward increasing human and civil rights, participants saw themselves as the latest in a string of marginalized groups who demanded and ultimately won equal rights.

The most frequent movement analogy was to the civil rights movement. Participants paralleled civil rights struggles of the 1960s to their own battles for gay and lesbian civil rights, including same-sex marriage. Some tied the campaign for same-sex marriage to the movement to eliminate laws against interracial marriage. Julie, a thirty-five-year-old project manager, is of Middle Eastern and white descent and is in an interracial relationship. Of her participation in the weddings, she said, "I thought a lot about racial history with marriage and the history of marriage in the United States. I was thinking about the history of racially mixed folks who weren't able to get married. So I feel like we're a continuation of that civil rights movement." The legacy of laws against interracial marriage also influenced Tim, a child of an interracial marriage, nurturing his interest in marriage equality. Respondents described their conviction that marriage equality was just a matter of time and that historical change was on their side: as marriage law had been revised over the last century, it would continue to adapt. They drew encouragement from the histories of other movements.

Marrying for the Cause

The San Francisco events were a unique occasion where political meaning dominated a social institution purportedly about love. For the majority of respondents, the weddings were an opportunity to challenge the assumption that marriage is the purview of only different-sex couples and wide-ranging discriminatory beliefs about lesbians and gays. Like Robert, they meant their actions to be understood as political statements. They were committing civil disobedience, doing what they had never before been allowed to do and insisting that they had a right to marriage.

The San Francisco weddings themselves were a place of protest. There, participants built a sense of collectivity, making that line one of the few in which people were non-adversarial: if they did not get a turn to marry, at least someone else did. In this way, the marriages were about the lesbian and gay movement, rather than a couple's benefits; they were about the group, not the individual. From the perspective of many respondents, the weddings mattered even without legal stature. They were an opportunity, as Terrance and Kelly noted, to communicate a loving, supportive—even "normal"—homosexuality to the world and to challenge negative assumptions of same-sex couples' deviance. They provided out same-sex couples with a venue to show those who were not out, be they young or old, that you can be happy and gay.

It took a village. Supportive city hall staffers and volunteers from all over the Bay Area made the weddings possible by facilitating a large volume of marriages in the early days. The encouragement from city dwellers of all walks of life as they passed the lines of hopeful couples, often handing out basic necessities that enabled the couples to continue their wait—and the near total lack of a coherent opposition to the weddings—kept the protest fires burning.

Broadly speaking, the politically inflected meanings respondents offered for their San Francisco weddings contested the unequal position of gays and lesbians in contemporary society. This was more than just a story about claiming access to marriage; participants in the Winter of Love described marrying as a way to assert the legitimacy of non-heteronormative identities. They existed, they led happy and fulfilling lives, and they deserved the dignity of recognition. Quite actively, in marrying, they aimed to contest heteronormativity. Participants asserted their right to be happy, healthy, and loved, regardless of sexual identity. They were protesting marriage's status as a heterosexual practice and the presumption that only heterosexual couples are "normal." These meanings for the marriages strongly challenge heteronormative assumptions about heterosexuality as a privileged status and dispute the characterization of lesbian and gay sexuality as deviant. In these ways, they walk in the footsteps of earlier challenges mounted by the gay and lesbian rights movement and, indeed, challenges by other movements on behalf of social justice.

CHAPTER 3

MARRYING FOR RIGHTS

The San Francisco marriages were not just about challenging hetero-normativity or the way marriage dispenses rights and props up nor-mativity. For many respondents, they were also about gaining access to the privileged status of being normative. In a seeming contradic-tion, even as they vehemently decried social systems that rewarded some kinds of relationships (different-sex relationships) but not oth-ers (their own), many respondents also coveted those rewards. When given the opportunity to gain access to the legal and social advantages of marriage, they jumped at the chance. They married to protest their exclusion from marriage and to contest the heteronormative status quo that rewarded some relationships but not others, but they also married *because* it was normative. Participants talked in practical terms about their desire to secure the legal benefits of marriage for their relationship, and they articulated their desire to participate in this social rite of passage because, after all, that's what people do.

Steven, age thirty-nine, grew up in Ohio, in an area that was not especially gay-friendly, but not overtly hostile either. Affable and social, Steven got along with his classmates and members of his community. He embraced the values of the place where he grew up, particularly around family. His own family was close. No one he knew of in his family tree had ever divorced. When Steven was young, he imagined his own future patterned after that of his parents: he would grow up, marry, start a family. Discovering he was gay in his late teens threat-ened to upset this plan. He said, "Probably one of the biggest struggles for me in coming out was going through a time where I thought that [being gay] meant that I wasn't going to have any of the same kind of marriage and family and things like that [that my parents and siblings had]. That was probably the most upsetting thing to me was not having the same thing as the rest of my family, 'cause I really held all of that up as being a great example and just the place that I was from." Marriage meant family, it meant community, and it meant belonging. But it also meant heterosexuality. When Steven realized he was gay, he believed marriage, family, and belonging were unavailable to him. Deeply discouraged about his future happiness, Steven dropped out of college: if he couldn't have it all, why bother?

After moving west, Steven began articulating his anger at a society that considered him "second-class." He grew comfortable with his sexual identity and increasingly contested social preferences for heterosexuals. The system was unfair and biased, in Steven's mind, and he participated in protests for gay rights whenever he could. Returning to the values of his youth, he refused to believe marriage was unavailable to him since he was gay. Indeed, he reincorporated his desire for marriage into his identity as a gay man, merging the expectations he grew up with into his sexual identity rather than accepting them as mutually exclusive: "It became one of my goals, again, at some point after I had gotten more comfortable with being out and stuff. Marriage, to me, gave me more of a way to fit in with the way that I was brought up and things like that—for me. Whether or not that fit in with what the original plan was, I don't know. But that was my way of coming back around to what was comfortable for me as a kid." Like Steven, just over half of my respondents talked about a desire for the status of marriage, despite the institution's history of excluding them.

In their stories, the normative power of marriage is preserved, even as same-sex couples marry. If marriage did not remain normative, they might not have been so keen on getting married. This meaning for marriage underscores what Jeffrey Weeks (2008) has called the appeal of being ordinary. Through the law's system of rewards as well as quasi-legal and social benefits, marriage is marked as the expected adult status of citizens. Effectively, it is a form of symbolic capital, in the Bourdieusian sense: the status of "married" is a socially valuable attribute that grants its holder both legal and social advantages. Without married status—without the symbolic capital that marriage affords—couples are precluded from a whole host of legal rights and are left out of normative definitions of "family" (Powell et al. 2010).[1]

In this chapter, I suggest that these benefits, and the desire to gain them, are tied to the achievement of normative status. Being married meant something legally and socially to many participants, and those meanings preserved marriage's status as a normative, organizing structure of American society. Although critics of the institution of marriage have cited its overarching power to dispense rights as evidence that marriage ought to be dismantled (Polikoff 2008), the drive for same-sex marriage shows no signs of undoing marriage. The same is true of judicial and legislative challenges of DOMAs. These challenges have not yielded the elimination of marriage for the provision of something more inclusive. Instead, they have called for the incorporation of same-sex couples into marriage. Part of the commonsense logic of preserving the institution of marriage while expanding its boundaries owes to its normative status: we cannot imagine society without it. But without such imagining, same-sex marriage mounts only a weak critique of heteronormativity, preserving contemporary meanings of marriage even as it includes gay and lesbian couples, and is unlikely to significantly disrupt the hegemony of heteronormativity.

MARRIAGE AS SYMBOLIC CAPITAL

Marriage is important both legally and socially, and its restriction to different-sex couples reifies heteronormativity. Legally, marriage comes with a host of rights and benefits. At the federal level alone, marriage comes with 1,138 rights (General Accounting Office 2004). Since gay and lesbian marriages are not recognized at the federal level, same-sex couples do not have access to the many benefits of state sanction that their different-sex counterparts do. Currently, citizenship proceedings for immigrants are expedited and notably simpler for spouses of US citizens. Rights of adoption, inheritance, and hospital visitation are afforded legal spouses but not unmarried couples. Couples who lack marital status, on average, pay significantly more taxes over their lifetimes than those who are married (Badgett 2001). And without marriage, unmarried couples with children experience a precarious legal status in which the law does not always recognize both partners as legal parents (Badgett 2001; Bernstein 2001; Dalton 2001). Looking beyond rights and responsibilities, some scholars have argued that access to marriage is a central component of citizenship (Kandaswamy 2008). Simply put, marriage is a vehicle for dispensing benefits from the state. Without marriage, couples cannot access those benefits.

Being legally married has other benefits that we might think about as quasi-legal. Although not formally dispensed by the state, benefits such as employer-sponsored health care and retirement are frequently provided based on relationships codified by the state. Since gay and lesbian couples are not able to legally marry and have the state recognize their families, many of these quasi-legal benefits are unavailable to them (Badgett 2001).

Socially, marriage offers legitimacy and social recognition. Marriage sanctions certain arrangements as families, marking them as normal (Bourdieu 1998). Marriage is also a central aspect of cultural legibility. In studies of different-sex marriage, scholars have pointed out that, although increasingly thought of as an individual act, marriage nonetheless retains potent symbolic and cultural power (Cherlin 2004). It has been constructed as a rite of passage such that, even as age of first marriage is delayed, most young people report that they expect to marry during their lifetime (Cohn et al. 2011). The necessity of marriage for social mobility has decreased, but it is still an aspired-to status that shifts the relationship between the couple and the larger social world (Cherlin 2004).

When same-sex couples are denied access to this institution, their social marginalization is perpetuated. Their non-normative status is brought into relief because of their inability to participate in standard rites of passages and mainstream social discourse. Chrys Ingraham (1999), for instance, argues that heterosexuals benefit from being able to invite coworkers and supervisors to wedding rituals, introducing a social component into professional relationships. Such casual social interaction can have positive workplace consequences. Without legal marriage, same-sex couples cannot similarly deepen professional relationships. Even as different-sex couples are opting for cohabitation over marriage, the exclusion of same-sex couples from marriage matters. Different-sex couples who elect not to marry are, in effect, making the individual choice to opt out. Same-sex couples who do not support the institution of marriage cannot do so. Not only can't they opt in, they cannot choose *not* to marry and thereby convey their disapproval of the institution.

The courts have recognized both the legal and the social importance of marriage. In the Massachusetts Supreme Judicial Court's majority decision in *Goodridge v. Department of Public Health* (798 N.E.2d 941 [Mass. 2003], 955), the court emphasized the legal benefits of marriage, stating, "The benefits accessible only by way of a marriage license are enormous, touching nearly every aspect of life and death." Similarly, the Hawaii Supreme Court in 1993 forwarded an argument of equal protection on the basis of sex in their ruling in favor of same-sex marriage.

California's 2008 decision in *In re Marriage Cases* (43 Cal.4th 757 [Cal. 2008]) recognized the social import of marriage. In the majority decision on the case that originated with the question of the constitutionality of the 2004 San Francisco weddings, the California Supreme Court ruled that barring gays and lesbians from the state institution of marriage is unconstitutional. This was not a decision motivated by the importance of legal rights, however, since in California law same-sex couples can enter domestic partnerships that entail virtually the same set of rights and responsibilities as civil marriage. The question before the court was thus not whether gays and lesbians should be able to enter into a government-sanctioned union with attendant benefits and responsibilities, but whether that union could be termed differently for same-sex couples (domestic partnership in California, civil unions in other states) than for different-sex couples (marriage). In a decision that cited the symbolic power of the word "marriage," the California Supreme Court ruled that same-sex couples must have access to the formal term "marriage" as long as different-sex couples do.

With its importance symbolically, both socially and legally, marital status can be usefully conceptualized as a form of symbolic capital. Symbolic capital is any form of capital—social, economic, cultural, and so on—understood to represent a socially valuable attribute (Bourdieu 2001). It operates, as do other forms of capital, within fields of social relations wherein the relative quantity possessed and successfully deployed by an individual determines his or her position and status within the field (Bourdieu and Wacquant 1992). In this case, married couples have higher status than unmarried couples. They have access to legal benefits and the social lexicon of family, while unmarried couples, despite their being identical in other ways to married couples (for example, commitment, financial interdependence), do not. This is not to say that married people inherently deserve higher status in contemporary society—the question of merit is irrelevant. What is relevant is the power of marital status to organize relations.

For participants in the San Francisco same-sex weddings, the social and legal benefits of marriage were often central motivating factors for their participation. The interviewees in my sample demonstrated a keen awareness of the normative benefits of marriage, citing meanings for marriage that recognized its cultural power over others and its obvious legal benefits. Just over half (N = 22; 52 percent) described a legal meaning for their participation in the San Francisco weddings, and a similar number (N = 23; 55 percent) invoked culture-based meanings that cited their perception of marriage as a social ritual. For these interviewees, marriage was socially established as a rite of passage that signified citizenship and full membership in society—and they wanted that for their relationship. In invoking legal and social meanings, respondents were centrally citing—and endorsing—the normative status conferred by marriage.

MARRIAGE'S PRACTICAL PURPOSES

The legal benefits of marriage were a highly enticing motivation for many of the people I interviewed. As Raine, the disabled retiree, explained, she did not travel from Northern California to wait eleven hours in line to make a commitment; she did it for legal rights: "I just wanted the legal opportunity, but it didn't change how I felt about what I was doing with this woman and this family that we've raised. Heck, if it took that to change it, it wouldn't have made it this far." As Raine suggests, the legal benefits of state-sanctioned marriage were a motivating force in respondents' decision to participate in the San Francisco wedding events. Respondents recognized the value of these benefits and frequently mentioned them in explanation for how they decided to get married.

Julie, the project manager, became interested in marriage because of the rights she could not access. For her, gay and lesbian couples should be granted legal rights because straight couples receive them. She explained, "I think that my overall sense of it is that I feel cheated. And I really feel the difference every time someone [straight] in my office is married. I really feel cheated. I really feel the sense that they're allowed something that I'm not allowed to have and that they have a special class." Steven similarly observed about marriage: "That's really where people get their rights. Married couples having so many more rights than single people or same-sex coupled people. Really, it's where all these other rights kind of come from." Like Raine, Steven married for the legal benefits, not to ensure commitment. In his interview, he went out of his way to emphasize that he married for rights, not because he did not already feel committed to Philip. After speaking of his strong desire for marriage, Steven turned to Philip and said, "I definitely didn't want you to think because I was needing to go to city hall that I didn't feel like we were already married. It really was that whole extension—some of it was just trying to be practical." For Terrance, because a non-legal ceremony did not come with legal benefits, he was not interested. Through two decades-long relationships, Terrance, now retired, had never wanted a commitment ceremony. Why would he, he argued, when it would be "a ceremony that we know doesn't change how we file our income tax, doesn't change the fact that we have to have living trusts and durable powers of attorney to protect each other, where a heterosexual couple who are getting married, as soon as they get married, all those rights are there for them." Marriage was about rights.

Respondents mentioned several specific rights allocated with marital status, including inheritance, medical visitation, parental rights, taxes, immigration, access to partner's benefits (for example, social security), and spousal protection in court. Some spoke from experience. For example, Ernesto, the health educator, related the story of being denied access to his partner in the hospital years earlier: "Just before we moved over here, my partner had surgery and they were wheeling him into an area to wait and I wanted to be with him because I could tell that he was very upset and worried about the surgery he was having. And the person came to me and said, and these were his very words, 'Are you a blood relative?' And I said, 'No.' And he said, 'Well, you cannot come in here.'" It is worth noting that Ernesto is

Latino and Tony is white, so they do not look like blood relatives. Partners of the same race might have been perceived as possibly related by blood and not have received the same scrutiny by hospital staff. In any case, that experience compelled Ernesto to think hard about the benefits of marriage. He wanted the legal document that stated that he and Tony, his partner, were a family: "To us marriage was really important because when you are not a blood relative and you don't have a wedding certificate, you are not considered family in many places."

In contrast, Sonia, the public employee, had not experienced difficulty without marriage, but had heard of difficulties other lesbian couples had encountered. She married for the legal protections of marriage:

> When we heard about the marriages being performed, we assumed that it would lend some form of protection in terms of medical decisions. We were planning to buy a house, so legal issues. We've heard a lot of horror stories of couples who had been together for an extended period of time. One becomes very ill or passes away and then the other one's family comes and says, "You're out of here." And so we wanted to set up a situation where we could be assured that that wouldn't happen. Not that our families were opposed to us being together, but sickness and death bring out the worst in people, and so we just decided we wanted some form of legal protection.

For many respondents, these benefits were their main reasons for getting married. Jeffrey, the retired physician, quipped, "Actually, I didn't need so much marriage, but I wanted all the 1,138 whatever."

Frank found out the hard way just how important marriage is. Shortly after his 2004 marriage to Henry was invalidated, Henry passed away. Frank, a seventy-year-old retiree, was left destitute, despite their efforts to protect each other. He said, "We had gone through a lot of stuff legally, trying to protect each other. We were registered domestic partners. I was on his insurance. We didn't know what would happen if he died. And now I know that it would all be cancelled. If we were a married couple, I would still get his benefits, see? But I don't, as a domestic partner."

Parents felt the legal importance of marriage particularly acutely. On the day she and Lal married, Sophie, a forty-year-old graduate student, was pregnant, about to go to her first ultrasound. Despite her feminist suspicions of marriage as a patriarchal institution and her personal experience as the child of divorce, her imminent motherhood caused her to rethink her opposition to marriage:

> I had mixed feelings on marriage. But, particularly because I was pregnant and we were planning to have a kid, I was really aware that we were really, really, really at risk as a lesbian couple preparing to have a child. We had to go through so many routes to approximate adoption stuff. It sucks. Our daughter was born upstairs in a birth tub in our house, and my partner was inside the birth tub and delivered her. [Our daughter] opened her eyes and looked into my partner's eyes. There's no way that she [Lal] is not a totally, full, 100 percent full parent to our little girl. But from a legal perspective she was absolutely zero parent when our daughter was born, and we had to go through second-parent adoption and we had to pay almost a thousand dollars to change our names so that we could be seen as a family.

To underscore Sophie's point, second-parent adoption costs for same-sex couples can range from about $1,000 to upwards of $3,000, depending on attorney's fees and costs for any required home visits. This puts second-parent adoption out of reach for some families, making establishing legal parenthood rights a privilege available only to those able to afford it. Further, although California permits second-parent adoption by unmarried, same-sex partners, other states have prohibited it, making it unavailable even for couples with means (Bennett and Gates 2004).[2] Legal marriage would eliminate the need for and cost of the legal actions required for same-sex couples to share parenting rights. And, as Sophie explained, it would make clear that both she and Lal were full parents to their daughter.

In Case It's Legal

Numerous respondents frankly admitted that they never expected the marriages to last, but others were not so sure and, at least in part, believed the licenses *might* remain legal. In case the marriages did stay legal, they wanted that legal status. As Steven said, "If there were going to be some benefits from this, I didn't want to *not* have those benefits."

Other respondents took actions as though the marriages would be upheld. Sandra, fifty years old and disabled, for example, had several copies made of her marriage certificate just in case it remained valid: "I figured, this is a legal document. If it does stick, there will undoubtedly be places that want to see it. So we had the original and the original copy and then we made a bunch of copies like this." Especially as the days turned into weeks and city hall continued to issue same-sex wedding licenses, Sandra increasingly believed the legality of the marriages might stick.

Anne, the artist, was cautiously optimistic that the marriages would remain legal. As the courts took up the question of whether Mayor Gavin Newsom had overstepped his authority, Anne described thinking, "Maybe, maybe it'll be legal, maybe. There was always that thing out there." She found herself thinking differently about her relationship now that it had legal status: "It definitely shifts when you think you have a legal document. I was ready to file our taxes jointly, check out all the things that we could do now, all these things. We could adopt, 'cause we're married. . . . I was ready to jump on all those things and see what we could get. Try to get insurance together. Try to get a house loan together." Robert, the physical therapist who married a lawyer, recognized that the marriages would probably not remain legal, but he thought that perhaps fairness would trump the finer points of the law. He said, "There was hope that it would, somehow, hold. Yes, the mayor didn't have the power to do it, but it was the right thing to do and congratulations to him."

Respondents described deciding to marry in case legal status remained for those lucky few who were able to get a marriage license. For instance, Chris, a thirty-two-year-old marketing manager, explained that he and Alan, a thirty-eight-year-old construction manager, rushed to city hall on the first day of weddings because they "believed that whoever was in that window of time [and got a license] could potentially be the ones legally married until they approve it for everyone else." They believed some marriages, even only a handful, would be legal, and they wanted their chance.

Laura, the disabled retiree, also believed that the marriages would retain at least limited legality. She did not believe city hall would be permitted to continue issuing same-sex marriage licenses, but she thought those already issued would be protected and she had faith in California as a gay-friendly state. She said, "I didn't expect that [the marriages were] going to be upheld, necessarily, but I guess I actually thought they might be for California." Since legal status was an option for her fifteen-year relationship with Elizabeth, Laura was not going to miss her chance, and the two lined up at city hall at their first opportunity.

Marriage as Unnecessary?

Others felt less urgency about achieving the legal benefits of marriage because they had already approximated marriage through legal contracts. Terrance and Jack, both retired, had completed extensive legal paperwork years earlier designed to protect their relationship and assets in the event of something unexpected, such as a medical emergency. Even though the contracts were expensive, neither thought twice about taking these steps. In Terrance's mind, this very paperwork made the need for legal marriage feel less intense.

> The reason why I say that marriage, up until this event, was sort of like an afterthought? Well, marriage between gay men or lesbians would not be legally binding, so the legal things that my partner and I had done prior to this marriage—the marriage effort—to be sure that our rights were protected were more binding than maybe some of the marriage certificates of heterosexuals. We've been so explicit in the legal drawing up of wills and documents and all this other kind of stuff. Because of that, I felt like we had done the homework to be sure that what we had already entered into was a binding relationship. If you look at marriage as a binding relationship, we'd already engaged in that process.

While couples with the means and desire could execute similar legal protections, Brian, the lawyer, recognized that not everyone could or would. He said, "We're fortunate. We have the power and the money to replicate marriage in a lot of ways in our own household. That is not true for the vast, vast majority of people."

Even though some felt secure in these legal maneuvers, others expressed doubts about the ability of contracts and wills to stand up in the absence of a marriage certificate. Sandra, for example, acknowledged the vulnerability she and her partner experience, even though her family is supportive of her relationship and they have undertaken numerous legal contracts. She said, "I don't care how many times you talk to a lawyer or whatever, if you're gay, there's always the chance that somebody in your family will decide that they need your stuff more than your partner does." Sandra suffers from a debilitating neurological disease and worries that Olivia, a forty-year-old programmer, will not be protected in the event that Sandra takes a significant turn for the worse. As her disease has made it more and more difficult for her to leave the house, she depends on Olivia to a greater extent. It breaks her heart to think that Olivia might not receive their house and her possessions should something happen to her.

Others cited different reasons for seeing legal approximations of marriage as unsatisfactory. Robert, the physical therapist, pointed out that while legal work may approximate some of the benefits of marriage, it cannot create all of them. He related a friend's experience as a non-US citizen in a committed relationship with a US citizen: "You hear these people say, 'Why do you want to get married? You can create all of those benefits that marriage provides through wills.' No. It's simply not true. And here's an example, our very dear friends, he flew over here on the off-chance that if they actually got married here that at some point down the road it would allow him to become a citizen and he could live here without all the hassle of dealing with immigration." For some rights, as the *Goodridge* decision stated, only a marriage license will do.

Considering the interview data of the participants in the San Francisco weddings, the legal rights–granting function of same-sex marriage helps explain the pressing desire by many respondents to get married immediately and evidences the utility of understanding marriage as symbolic capital. By being denied access to marriage, same-sex couples are denied a degree of mobility in society. Gaining access to those legal rights was important enough that people waited in line for hours and even days for their opportunity to legally protect their relationship.

Gaining Social Recognition

The legal benefits alone, however, did not cover the institutional meanings respondents assigned to their participation; they also cited decidedly social meanings for marriage. Many of my respondents characterized marriage as a standard social institution that they expected, at one time or another, to participate in. Raine explained, synthesizing an argument several respondents voiced, "That's what people do. That's what heterosexual couples do to show that level of commitment: they take that legal jump and that's what says to everyone how we feel about each other." Marriage marked an important step in the life continuum, a site of transition into adulthood. Elizabeth, the accounting assistant, cited the fairy tale narrative of the white wedding: "That's what we thought you do. When you grow up and you fall in love, you get married." Diana, the administrative assistant, termed marriage the culmination of the "natural course of a relationship."

Of course, many of my respondents recognized at some point in their lives that being gay has historically meant not being able to marry (Weston 1991). In addition to understanding this experience as one of psychological strain on the individual—or minority stress (Riggle and Rostosky 2007)—respondents described it as an exclusion from culture. Stanley, a fifty-six-year-old software engineer, explained, "It is quite a thing to realize how cut-off we've been from one of the central dreams and hopes in our culture: getting married. I think I certainly didn't realize how cut-off we were from that until we were actually able to do it." Even as lesbians and gays were unable to access this central cultural ritual, they were nonetheless expected to participate in the family rituals of others. Having attended weddings throughout their lives, many participants pointedly felt their exclusion from this ritual. Stanley's partner, Craig, the research manager, explained, "I was tired of going to other people's weddings. It gets to be a little fatiguing after a while. When you get that wedding invitation in the mail and it's like, 'Oh, great. Good for them. However [we can't marry]!' So I tended not to go to weddings unless it was somebody really close or it was one where the marriage license was not going to be signed."

The consequences of the social exclusion of lesbians and gays from marriage are significant. Brian de Vries and colleagues have argued that the cultural exclusion of lesbians and gays from marriage explains the up to 13 percent higher rate of singlehood among this population (de Vries 2007; de Vries et al. 2009): when gays and lesbians are excluded from marriage, they do not seek "marriageable" partners (see also

Green 2006). Other scholars have suggested that the lower relation-ship longevity—and associated higher rate of singlehood—among lesbians and gays stems from the lack of social and legal support for these commitments, not to mention society's general condemnation and silencing of same-sex relationships (Auchmuty 2004).

Not all respondents acquiesced to the heteronormative assump-tion that marriage was only for different-sex couples. Like Steven, some respondents worked through those feelings of exclusion and decided to resist them. Lois, a forty-two-year-old physical therapist, explained, "We knew that we were going to get married. There was no question that we were going to get married. Marriage, to us, was just really important. . . . You dream all your life about getting married and then you realize you're gay and you think, okay, that's never going to happen. But for us, we always wanted that. So marriage in general we knew we were going to do." This story is actually quite common. Kath Weston (1991) finds in her study of gays' and lesbians' chosen families that after a period of transition and often extreme isolation follow-ing coming out, gays and lesbians build and participate in what can only be called families, disputing the equation of homosexuality with non-procreation and the absence of commitment. Although many respondents initially associated being gay with an exclusion from marriage, not all preserved this association. Many, instead, resisted the assumption that being gay meant being single. More importantly, many resisted the assumption that being gay meant exclusion from American culture's desirable rite of passage: marriage.

Following the logic of Lois and Steven, many interviewees saw mar-riage as a way to experience social legitimacy. Marriage eliminated the felt tension between cultural acceptance and sexual identity. Through legal marriage, lesbian and gay couples sought to be gay—perhaps even more openly so—and be recognized as partners. As Frank summed it up, he and Henry married after fifty years together "for acceptance, for acknowledgement, to be acknowledged by people. . . . I think the recognition, first and foremost, was important to us." Some couples, including Lois and Carrie and Steven and Philip, explained that they experienced this acceptance at the familial or community level through non-legal commitment ceremonies. As Kathleen Hull (2006) and Ellen Lewin (1998) have shown, commitment ceremonies have been used as tools by lesbian and gay couples to negotiate their exclusion from the state-sanctioned institution, establish family and community ties, and emphasize the authenticity of their relationships.

Explicitly, marriage was tied to the definition of family for many respondents. Marnie, the accountant, explained, "If marriage has any constant, it's that it's in some way embedded in family. For me, it's embedded in family." Terrance, too, saw the San Francisco marriages as a way to access the language of family, despite his own caution about allowing the state to have a say in his relationship: "I think it maybe spoke to a lot of people who get [the concept of] a family, saying what family's about. This is another way of owning family, owning the word 'family.' Because maybe the many gay men and lesbians who you talk to who go back to their siblings' weddings and their siblings' ceremonies and they have never been able to have one of those for themselves. I think it spoke to people who had a strong sense of family." Marriage was a way to gain legitimacy in using common social discourse about family and relationships. This resonated strongly with Aaron, a twenty-nine-year-old attorney. He explained that, putting aside its legal meaning, marriage allowed him to authentically use the term "husband," a term he felt had explanatory value like no other. He appreciated its ability to convey his and Gabe's relationship quickly. He said, "Being married, saying 'husband,' just as a matter of social discourse, it allows me to shortcut an explanation of who this person is and who I am and what we are. So I say 'husband' and they know they have to invite us both to a dinner party. I say 'husband' [and] they know that we live together and all these things."

Establishing Social Relationships through Law

Other couples more ardently cited the legal aspect of the weddings in San Francisco as generating a feeling of social legitimacy. For instance, Raine and Isabel committed to each other in a ceremony two years after they met, but rushed to San Francisco's city hall four years later all the same. Isabel, the professor, explained, "I thought, wow, wouldn't that be wonderful to be able to legally legitimize what's been going on for so long between us. I wanted to be part of it. I just wanted to be part of the whole gathering of people. When I got home [the day the weddings started] and saw the images of the people that were being married, I was just like, 'I want that.' Marriage was really stressed in the culture I grew up in. Legally it does mean something. And emotionally it means something, too, I think. We had a commitment ceremony right after we got together, but this was different."

Raine, too, explained that the legal component of the wedding—the state sanction—was important. She said, "It was about being able to legitimize and to have that moment to stand in front of someone that speaks those words and we get to say the same words like every other couple ever got to say and have that moment—'cause it's really about that moment for everyone and that certificate." Legal marriage, having their relationships endorsed by the state, offered a unique opportunity for lesbian and gay couples—and individuals—to be recognized as authentic in the same way that different-sex couples have long been recognized.

As Judith Butler (2005) poignantly argues in discussing the traumatic life of the patient of John Money's known variously as David and Brenda, in order to enjoy the status of human, we must be legible in existing cultural discourses. Butler argues that this individual was unable to be clearly man or woman and, as such, found himself (the pronoun he preferred) unintelligible in a culture that presumes gender as a priori. Unintelligible, David/Brenda was illegitimate; he was without gender and thus could not be understood in the existing social discourse of personhood. Although in not as stark terms, gays and lesbians often find their relationships illegible in cultural discourse because they lack access to an institution tied to cultural citizenship. For many respondents, the San Francisco weddings allowed them to have their relationships fully recognized.

Marriage as Inclusive

Wedding made Sophie, the graduate student, feel like a true part of the larger community, not just her own chosen community, and it forced her to "grow up." She explained, "I felt the kind of entrance into a contract with my community when I said 'I do' in that context, that I realized that marriage is a social contract that binds people in a mutual accountability with a larger community, with our neighborhoods, with our schools, with our families, with the people that witness us. It was the contract. And I felt like I had to grow up, quite a bit, actually, to stand there. I cry every time I think about it." In citing her marriage as a catalyst for personal growth, Sophie located her experience of marriage in her responsibilities to her broader community, underscoring the way in which marriage produces citizens (Richardson 2003).

The San Francisco weddings marked a time many respondents felt entirely a part of society. For Barbara, despite her far leftist leanings and personal rejection of marriage as a social institution, the experience nonetheless served to impact her feeling of social legitimacy as a lesbian: "I have to say, by the end of those two days, I felt rather validated by society as a whole." Elizabeth, too, experienced some ambivalence about her newfound sense of inclusion but noted that it was explicitly about her relationship to the outside culture, not to her partner, Laura: "But I have to say, for me, it suddenly felt legitimate. And I wasn't sure if that was a good thing or not. A lot of my self-definition has been built on being other, being outsider. And to suddenly feel legitimate was like, wow [laughs]. But it didn't change us and our relationship 'cause we already felt married." Brian, the lawyer, put it most succinctly when he said, "You know when you feel somewhat disconnected from the culture and then all of a sudden connected to the culture? I don't know what the word is for that. But that was my feeling, anyway." Feeling safe and accepted for who they were, respondents felt a part of society itself, experiencing inclusion. That experience changed how many participants related to society more generally.

Isabel's transformation was among the most profound as she waited among the throngs of people outside city hall. Interestingly, it was not the actual marriage itself that changed her, but the promise of it. She said, "I felt less—I don't know if 'sinful' is the right word. I felt less of an outsider. I felt like I have nothing to be ashamed of. I haven't done anything wrong. And I think, up to that point, I felt somewhere inside that I had done something wrong or was doing something wrong." Raine, Isabel's partner, elaborated on Isabel's comment, "Like almost a living-in-sin kind of thing was still haunting her, in a way." Then Isabel, looking fondly at Raine, completed her thought:

> But that changed before the actual marriage happened—it was in the line on the way. The marriage didn't change it, just the experience of being with all those committed-to-each-other normal people. You know what I mean? Just everyday, average family people.

And I just thought, wow, this is so okay. 'Cause it had never felt
wrong. One thing that blew my mind is as I was getting closer to
her and farther away from my ex-husband and committing what
would be certainly classified by [the religion I was brought up in]
as sin, it never felt wrong. And that always blew my mind 'cause I'd
been taught when you stepped outside of certain boundaries there
would be immediate consequences, that you would feel bad about
what you were doing. And it just never felt that way. Never.

Following the marriages, Isabel was more secure in her identity and,
she explained, able to commit that much more of herself to Raine. By
losing her fear of social sanction, Isabel was able both to make herself
more vulnerable and to feel empowered.

Although same-sex couples have been excluded from legal marriage, their lack of access to this status does not exclude them from
aspects of society where marriage matters. It is worth noting that the
data used here were collected from individuals who were part of couples at the time of the wedding events and thus had a particular kind
of stake—perhaps a more immediate and personal stake—in access
to marriage. However, if we think of marriage as symbolic capital, it
exists as both held and potential capital. The potential to accumulate
capital—an individual's possible trajectory—is meaningful in establishing his or her social position (Bourdieu and Wacquant 1992). Supporting this argument, studies of attitudes toward later life among
lesbian and gay individuals, analyzed in relation to their state-of-
residence's policies, or lack thereof, on recognizing same-sex relationships have similarly shown that state recognition impacts both single
and coupled individuals and affects both their current quality of life
and their future plans (de Vries et al. 2009). Even those excluded from
marriage are implicated in it.

PREVIOUSLY MARRIED PARTICIPANTS

Not all of my respondents had always been excluded from marriage,
and their prior experience "on the inside" influenced their desire for
marriage to their same-sex partner. Five women and one man in my
sample had been legally married before. Their age range was broad,
from Deirdre at thirty-seven to Jeffrey at sixty-three, with some

divorces happening only a few years prior to the San Francisco weddings, suggesting that these experiences are not an artifact of a generation forced into the closet in order to be able to become parents (Lewin 1998; Weston 1991). The experience of the ease of marital privilege echoed in these six respondents' minds as they participated in their legal same-sex ceremony.

Deirdre, the writer, explained, "I was married to a man before, so I have a particularly strong reaction: wait, I'm the same person but my rights have changed because my partner's different? I don't get that. . . . It makes absolutely no sense to me that my current relationship is not supported as much as my past relationship was. And I have a strong sense of entitlement because I lived as a straight person for twenty-eight years or whatever. I feel very strongly about that." Marital privilege, for these respondents, was about being recognized as a couple.

Raine, for instance, was sensitive to the difference between how her relationship with Isabel was recognized and how her family reacted to her previous three heterosexual marriages, despite the fact that none of those three had lasted as long as her relationship with Isabel.

> I was talking to my sister just yesterday and I was taking a stand about our [Isabel and my] relationship because they're wanting me to come back for my parents' fiftieth wedding anniversary, and I said, "Not again, not without Isabel." And my sister was, "Well, I knew this was coming." And I'm like, you know, you wouldn't expect that I would show up without my husband. I said, "I have been with her for fucking eight years. When are you guys going to get that?" I've never, I mean, I was married three times [and] never was I with a person that long. I said, "I've been with her for eight fucking years. Don't you think it's about time?" And they're like, "It's been that long? You've been with her that long?"

In fact, when Isabel and Raine met, they were both married to men. They met in church, became close friends, and eventually got romantically involved. For both, this was their first relationship with a woman.

As their relationship grew, Isabel, too, became increasingly attuned to their exclusion from social recognition, juxtaposing their relationship's lack of access with different-sex marriages, her own included, that were less serious about commitment. She said, "Marriage was something that I had done with my ex that never meant as much as what I couldn't do with her. I would get so pissed off when they'd be talking about Britney Spears, who had her one-week-long marriage. Fifty-five hours. I mean, you know. Or J. Lo with her three. We've been together for so long and couldn't have that."[3] Nonetheless, these comparisons did not compel Isabel to doubt marriage as an institution. Despite her personal dissatisfaction with her first marriage and the bad examples of marital relationships she had witnessed, Isabel still embraced the power of the institution and wanted it for herself and Raine:

> Some see marriage as an outdated institution, but I want marriage. I don't want a civil union because that's like saying you're different enough that we can't give you those rights, because only a certain part of the population deserves those rights. . . . You can't help but think of your parents when you think of marriage. And how pretty it can *not* be sometimes [laughs]. But, I mean, we've both been married. I was married to one guy. Raine was married to three different ones. It wasn't like this was our first marriage, but it was the first one for me that was based on love, not on obligation.

Like Isabel, other previously married respondents carefully distinguished between the ideal of marriage and their experience of it, arguing that their previous marriages were less validly marriages than their current relationships. Isabel was entirely in love with Raine, and Raine with her, consistent with the ideal of marriage. Armed with these experiences, they felt particularly affronted that their relationship was not state recognized. They demanded that law and culture recognize their commitments.

The experience of being previously married encouraged these respondents to argue for the revision of marriage's boundaries but, pointedly, not its definition. They embraced marriage as an institution and the legal and social benefits it affords as they challenged the social understanding of marriage as an exclusively heterosexual practice. They did not seek to replicate a two-sexed relationship, nor did they demand changes to the institution of marriage. Simply put, they called for a revision of *who* can marry, but not of the institution of marriage itself.

A Weak Critique of Heteronormativity

In citing the benefits of normativity, participants characterized marriage as a protective shield from homophobic institutions and individuals, one that could facilitate everything from institutional interactions to respect for a partnership. Marriage would have ensured Ernesto could visit his partner in the hospital and forced outsiders to see Sophie, Lal, and their daughter as a family unit. It would put Sandra's mind at peace that, no matter what happens to her, Olivia is financially protected. As a presumed part of the life course, marriage is socially constructed as an inevitability, both normal and natural, and several of my respondents aspired to it. They grew up expecting to marry and experienced at least a brief period of personal struggle when marriage seemed unavailable to them because of their sexual identity.

Although marriage is often thought of as a private commitment, its individual value and satisfaction are always read through a larger social lens. As Isabel noted, marriage is stressed in many cultures. Marriage is a union designed to dispense legal rights and to orient the behavior of others through the deployment of social meaning. It gave Aaron the language to explain his relationship to Gabe. These stories underscore that marriage is not just about the two people who say their vows but about being able to move through society in legible ways. Marriage offered respondents access to the social discourse of relationships. These stories suggest that there is something attractive about being ordinary that underlies the drive for same-sex marriage (Weeks 2008).

This consideration of the ways normative marriage makes life better for some same-sex couples complicates our understanding of the meanings participants in the San Francisco weddings ascribed to their unions. Many did want to contest heteronormativity through marrying. But many—some of the same respondents, in fact—also wanted to preserve much of marriage's normative status, if only so that they could leverage its benefits. Indeed, over three-fourths of respondents who cited a political meaning for their participation *also* offered either a social or legal reason, or both, as well. Their stories detail how the benefits of marriage are intensely compelling, offering everything from financial simplicity for couples to social legitimacy.

Instead of calling for broad changes to the institution of marriage, in invoking meanings for marriage grounded in its normative status, these respondents demanded only an expansion of who it admits: same-sex marriage was about inclusion, not social revolution. They sought to remake the meaning of marriage into one available to any couple, regardless of sex, weakly critiquing the heterosexuality of the institution. These respondents critiqued the boundaries around participation in marriage but did not question the social value of marriage itself. Indeed, they demanded marriage explicitly *for* its social value. Insofar as marriage is presumed to be between members of different sexes, the assertion that same-sex couples deserve the right to marry challenges the presumption that marriage is a heterosexual institution (Calhoun 2000). It does not, however, push on the institution to unpack its system of privilege (Duggan 2003; Ettelbrick 1992).

Respondents' citation of legal and social meanings for marriage embraced marriage as an institution and the benefits it affords, even as they challenged the social understanding of marriage as an exclusively heterosexual practice. They did not seek to replicate a two-sexed relationship, but demanded access to its privileges, calling for a revision of *who* can marry, but not of the institution of marriage itself. These contentions constitute a weak critique of heteronormativity in marriage. They hold the potential to disrupt marriage's definition as a heterosexual practice but still preserve the assignment of privilege and normative status to married couples. Whether same-sex marriage can undermine heteronormativity broadly is not guaranteed or even implied in the invocation of legal and social meanings for marriage.

CHAPTER 4

MARRYING FOR LOVE

In Robert's mind, marrying in San Francisco was about making a political statement. In Steven's mind, it was about securing legal and social recognition for his relationship. For most of my respondents, these two meanings for marriage resonated strongly. They wanted to challenge the unequal social position they found themselves in because of heteronormativity and, simultaneously, many wanted to gain the privileges marriage bestows. In complicated ways, these individuals acknowledged the presumption of heterosexuality and the social preferences for normative behavior, sometimes pushing against this system and sometimes wanting to be on the inside. Separate from these, a final set of meanings for marriage that cropped up in my interviews ignored normativity all together, insisting that same-sex couples are no different from different-sex couples. In these descriptions of marriage, marriage is (only) about love.

About one-third of respondents explained their participation as stemming from a general cultural expectation that, simply put, when you love someone, you get married, regardless of whether they are the same sex as you or a different one. These participants echoed the contemporary meanings for marriage commonly found among different-sex couples, including the belief that marriage is about emotional satisfaction (Giddens 1991), personal achievement (Cherlin 2004), and finding oneself (Bellah et al. 2008). This suggests that gay couples have much in common with their committed straight counterparts. Some advocates of marriage equality have embraced the apparent similarity of meanings for marriage across different sexual identities, arguing that same-sex marriage should be legal because gay and lesbian couples are *just like* straight couples. This framing is consistent with strategic moves by the gay and lesbian movement historically to emphasize their similarity to, rather than difference from, the straight majority (Bernstein 1997; Bernstein and Taylor 2013a) and fits into a broader set of assimilationist politics (Ghaziani 2011). The invocation of love and commitment as meanings for marriage among same-sex couples should not be a surprise. These are the contemporary cultural norms for marriage and, as with all cultural norms, have influence beyond just those able to marry (Swidler 2001). Examining this borrowing helps us trace the influence of cultural norms and illustrates the extent to which norms established for heterosexual marriage have permeated definitions of marriage among those excluded from the institution.

As with the other meanings for marriage offered by respondents, the idea of marrying for love did not occur in a vacuum; these individualistic understandings of marriage appeared alongside political, social, and legal meanings for the weddings. But, unlike the other meanings for marriage discussed so far, they were not accompanied by an engagement with heteronormativity. By avoiding the concept of heteronormativity all together in this meaning for marriage, this argument effectively asserts that (some) gay and lesbian couples *are* normative. In so doing, this strategy ultimately circumvents but does not destabilize heteronormativity. In her analysis of legal successes by the gay and lesbian movement, Mary Bernstein (2001) argues that campaigns that preserve heteronormativity are more successful, leading us to interpret this focus on love as a potentially winning strategy.

However, I suggest it may win the battle but not the war. Positioning same-sex couples as "the same" as heterosexual couples risks reinforcing, rather than undermining, heteronormativity. Such framing tacitly accepts a (heteronormative) standard of coupledom that does not impact the broader systems of inequality produced by heteronormativity. Instead, as Celia Kitzinger and Sue Wilkinson (2004) argue about claims that gay parents are the same as straight parents, it papers over ways in which the lived experience of being gay (or being a gay parent) matters in the experience of marriage (and parenting). In this chapter, I discuss the ways marriage equality advocates invoked a meaning for marriage grounded in love and some participants' support for this understanding of marriage. But, I suggest, even as this shared meaning for marriage exists as part of a cultural norm for marriage, it is fundamentally false: gay couples are not the same as straight couples. To this point, I offer evidence from respondents' experiences in city hall applying for licenses, evidence that illustrates ways in which same-sex marriage, in fact, is not like different-sex marriage, including the length of the lines, the materials given each couple by city hall, and even the application form itself. When the narrative about same-sex marriage ignores these differences, it fails to disrupt heteronormativity.

Just Like Anyone Else

In what has been characterized as a liberal, rights-based discourse (Green 2010), proponents of same-sex marriage have embraced marriage as an institution that can confer a range of benefits on gay and lesbian couples, from hospital visitation to spousal privilege in court to inheritance, ultimately serving as a watershed right that will dismantle barriers between heterosexuals and homosexuals and demonstrate that we are all just people. In this line of argument, legal same-sex marriage will undo what is now effectively "second-class citizenship" for gay and lesbian couples (Wolfson 2004).

Historical antecedents to the mobilization of "love" as the most important component of marriage and family include the 1987 Gay and Lesbian March on Washington. As Kath Weston (1991) documents, speakers repeatedly grounded their claim to LGBT rights, couples' rights, and parenting rights in the claim that love was all that was needed.

At the time of the Winter of Love, same-sex marriage advocates in the Bay Area frequently adopted this liberal, rights-based argument. Molly McKay, cofounder of Bay Area–based Marriage Equality California (MECA), cited the similarity between gay and straight couples in her rationale for the annual Freedom to Marry Day marriage counter actions. In these actions, gay and lesbian couples around the country go to their local marriage counter on or around Valentine's Day, request a marriage license, and are denied. She experiences these annual protests as emotionally compelling; she explained, "[They were] a great opportunity to talk to all the other couples who were standing in line to get married, the straight couples, who really got to see all the commonality. You know, we were feeling the same feelings

they were feeling: we were excited; it was scary; it was thrilling; all
of those things we shared—how we met, all those stories. So by the
time we got up to the front of the line, they would get the license, no
questions asked, and we would be turned away, and they would really
get it, like in a deep, symbolic way, what that might feel like to us."
McKay argued that she and her partner came to the marriage counter
for the same reasons as straight couples. They share the same desire
for commitment but are refused because of a discriminatory law. By
enacting this experience for an audience of straight couples, McKay
and other marriage counter protesters emphasized the similarities
between straight and gay couples.

In their 2007–2008 television ad campaign, Equality California
(EQCA), the other prominent marriage equality organization in the
Bay Area, sounded much the same note: gay and lesbian couples are
the same as heterosexual couples. Seth Kilbourn, policy director of the
Equality California Institute, explained:

> [The ads] basically ask the question to the average Californian, "What
> if you were prohibited from marrying the person that you love? How
> would that impact your life? How would that make you feel? How
> would that change the way that you approach life?" And then, by ask-
> ing that question, [we] remind people that there's an entire group of
> people who are excluded from marrying the person that they love. So
> imagine how you would feel if you couldn't marry the person that
> you love. Well, there's an entire group of people out there who are
> prevented from marrying the person that they love every single day.

Kilbourn characterized the opposition to same-sex marriage as stemming from a general misunderstanding about lesbian and gay couples.
He explained, "[The general public is] not sure that gay and lesbian
people take their relationships as seriously as non-gay people do." And
thus, his work as an activist is to help them see that gay and lesbian
people "have the same level of commitment, the same kind of love for
their partners as non-gay people do." Indeed, in thinking back on the
impact of the 2004 San Francisco weddings, EQCA's executive director
Geoff Kors highlighted the way the events showed gays and lesbians
as no different from heterosexuals: "I think for the first time people
around the world saw lesbian and gay couples as being just like them."

History provides evidence of the strengths of such strategic deployments of sameness. Looking at the gay and lesbian rights movement, Bernstein (1997) notes ways in which it has emphasized similarities between a gay identity and a straight identity in particular campaigns. She argues that this is a strategic collective action, designed to persuade the straight majority to meet the demands of the gay and lesbian rights movement. It has a track record of success, too. Brian Powell and colleagues (2010), too, suggest that tactics promoting marriage equality that emphasize similarities between same-sex families and different-sex families—particularly about the shared experience of raising children—are more likely to sway the American public.

However, critiques of these "normalizing constructions" (Clarke 2002) also exist. In their critique of frameworks of advocacy for same-sex marriage, Kitzinger and Wilkinson (2004) take on another claim by liberal advocates of lesbian and gay rights: the claim that gay parents are just like straight parents. Kitzinger and Wilkinson show that the psychology literature does not find that gay and lesbian parents are equivalent to straight parents, as many advocates of lesbian and gay parenting rights have argued. In fact, research has found that the children of lesbian and gay parents *are* different from those of straight parents (Berkowitz 2009; Stacey and Biblarz 2001): they are less likely to conform to normative sex and gender roles, more willing to explore nontraditional gender activities and occupations, and more likely to report having or being open to homoerotic relationships. And yet, the gay and lesbian rights discourse maintains defensive frames that construct gay families as "just like" any other family.

In terms of marriage, it is an open question whether gay and lesbian couples experience their relationships as being just like heterosexual relationships. Data from my interviews suggests that, in important ways, respondents did perceive their relationships as consistent with cultural expectations about (different-sex) marriage. As I detail below, the status description of "married" resonated with many respondents. About a third of my interviewees talked about marriage in explicit terms similar to those used to describe contemporary different-sex marriage. But these meanings are best understood as cultural borrowings of themes about love and marriage (Swidler 2001), rather than strategic framings. Further, their comparatively low rates of invocation compared to political, legal, and social meanings for marriage suggest that a strategic argument about same-sex couples as just like straight couples has significant limitations.

ALREADY MARRIED

While advocates have emphasized similarities between same-sex and different-sex couples in their love for their partners and their desire for formalized commitment, several respondents echoed this similarity claim in a different way. They asserted that even before the San Francisco weddings, for all intents and purposes, they were already married. These respondents effectively insisted that they were equivalent to different-sex married couples in their lived experience of coupledom.

By "already married," respondents meant that their partnerships met the conventional expectations of a marriage: they had a long-term commitment and were sharing a home, family responsibilities, and financial responsibilities. In all but name, they were married. For example, when prompted to explain his use of "already married," Tim, the policy analyst, said, "When I say 'as married,' if you think of, aside from the act of marriage, what identifies in people's minds when a couple is—I'm making air quotes—'married,' we were all those things. We had been living together for seventeen years. We'd been completely part of each other's families, completely part of each other's—we don't even have separate circles of friends. Part of everything about each other; we were completely intertwined. . . . Our finances are completely merged. I don't know. Our lives are just completely shared. I'm not actually sure what else to say." Tim's explanation was similar to those of several other respondents who pointed to the interdependence of their and their partners' lives. Tim explained his meaning more succinctly moments later: "We are each other's family. We are each other's closest relative. I think that's another way to think of it."

Diana, the administrative assistant, ticked off criteria generally assigned to different-sex marriage to explain why she defined her eight-year relationship with Mia as a marriage. They had "monogamy, marrying of finances and households, raising kids together, support emotionally and financially—everything I grew up thinking marriage meant." Janet and Cynthia, together twelve years when they married, used the "already married" phrase when I spoke to them as well. With good humor, Janet, the nurse, explained that she meant they were "committed to each other, living our lives together, sharing the good and the bad and the ugly."

It was not that respondents misunderstood the legal status of marriage. Kelly, the professor, emphasized that her use of the phrase "already married" did not mean she and Michelle, a forty-one-year-old accountant, together eight years when they wed in city hall, were married in the legal sense, "but we had the other non-legal part of marriage: commitment for life." Like Kelly, interviewees underscored the cultural meaning of marriage in defining their pre-wedding relationships as marriage.

With eleven years of commitment prior to his San Francisco wedding, when Robert, the physical therapist, said "already married," he meant that he and Brian were, in a word, "joined." He elaborated, "We complement each other. The two of us make a whole. It also means being committed to each other and, in our mind, being monogamous and supporting each other and loving one another, all that good stuff." Brian, the lawyer, spoke in similar terms of their close connection to each other. He said, "We're very much integrated. I mean, we hardly are ever apart. I think the whole time we've been together, Robert's had to go to Southern California or somewhere that I couldn't go and maybe we've slept apart a few nights in all these years." This closeness to Brian was what the practice of marriage meant: it meant emotional interdependence and physical closeness. Brian and Robert already had that. In the colloquial sense, they were married.

Among my respondents, the average relationship length at the time of marriage was ten years, with fifteen respondents (over one-third of the sample) reporting relationships longer than ten years and nine (over one-fifth of those I interviewed) reporting relationships in excess of fifteen years. One couple had been in a committed relationship for over fifty years at the time of their marriage, as had the well-publicized first couple to be granted a marriage license, Del Martin and Phyllis Lyon. These couples were in committed, dyadic relationships.

It was not just time together, however, that made couples see themselves as already married. For example, Julie, the project manager, described marriage as a relationship where you work out problems.

Thinking about her shared experiences with Addy, she saw their commitment as very deep. She explained that she used the phrase "already married" because "we're very emotionally dependent. We'd been through a lot together, even though we'd only been together for three years. We'd been through a lot of hardships together that had bonded us together."

For others, the encouragement to consider themselves married came from a singular—and joyous—event. Among those who held commitment ceremonies, these formal occasions stood in for legal weddings, creating the feeling they were married. As Philip, the retail company project coordinator, explained, his ceremony with Steven in 2003 made them a married couple, whether or not they had the legal opportunity during the Winter of Love. He said, "In my eyes, we had gone through our wedding ceremony already and that time was our time that we got married. I didn't think that we would have to go in again to get married. In my eyes, we were already married. It didn't matter if it was legal, not legal, not valid, or whatever. In my eyes, it just meant we were married." Alan and Chris, together eight years at their San Francisco marriage, felt similarly. Four years prior to their city hall wedding, the two held a commitment ceremony, attended by over one hundred people. Alan explained, "That was our commitment to each other and that was our marriage." Although he and Chris were excited about the city hall opportunity, Alan did not need that experience in order to feel married. He said, "It was great that it happened. But I wasn't sitting around longing for the day we could run down to city hall and get married 'cause it didn't matter to me because we were already married."

The frame of already married was applied to these couples by others as well. For years, Brian reported, "People would say, 'You're so married!' when they'd see us together." Marnie's family treated her and Phyllis "like every other married couple." Keith's young niece assumed Keith and Tim were married because that is how their relationship was treated in her family. Indeed, she was underwhelmed by their San Francisco wedding because she did not see how it changed anything.

It was not just family and close friends who interpreted these relationships as marriages. For instance, Ernesto's boss was unsurprised to learn he had married in the first days of the weddings because of her assessment of Ernesto's relationship. Ernesto, the health educator, recalled, "Well, I remember my boss saying, 'You know, I was thinking this is perfect for you and Tony because you are such a married couple already, you know. I was just thinking, I was wondering when you were going to say you're going to do this.'"

Many of the couples who married in San Francisco had years of commitment under their belts when they applied for a marriage license. Before their marriages were legal, they felt "married." Their explanations for this felt experience, despite a lack of legal sanction, largely drew on framings of marriage as about commitment, interdependency, and love. The actions of others in recognizing these couples as "married," too, were built on signals about the long-term commitment a couple had demonstrated. These applications of the concept of marriage are consistent with contemporary meanings for marriage among different-sex couples (Coontz 2005). No longer a required means of achieving social status and life success, marriage is increasingly identified by scholars of marriage and the family as a tool of the individual. That is, marriage is increasingly individualistic. Contemporary marriage is a capstone (Cherlin 2004; Coontz 2004) or a means to extended self-discovery (Bellah et al. 2008). In essence, it is an opportunity for individual expression that is simultaneously shared with a partner. Thus respondents' use of the phrase "already married" makes sense.

TALK OF LOVE AND MARRIAGE

Respondents demonstrated other ways in which they understood marriage similarly to different-sex couples in offering meanings for their same-sex marriages. In my interviews, respondents echoed many of the same meanings that the general population ascribes to marriage: as about love, commitment, and self-discovery. Over one-third (N = 15) offered such individualistic explanations for their desire to participate in the institution of marriage. For them, marriage was a means of preserving or securing intimacy and was important almost solely for the couple, not for the broader community. This is consistent with other work finding that gay and lesbian couples' motivations for marriage are more similar to than different from those of different-sex couples (Badgett 2009; Herdt and Kertzner 2006).

For some respondents, committing to marriage was the culminating step of a loving relationship, evidence of their love, and a means to self-knowledge (Bellah et al. 2008). Throughout their interview, Addy and Julie repeated the mantra that marriage is about love—and nothing else. The two come from very different class and race backgrounds. Addy was raised in foster care in low-income households, while Julie was raised upper middle class. Both Addy and Julie identify as biracial, Addy as white and Native American and Julie as Middle Eastern and white. Explicitly devaluing social structures of prejudice and inequality, Addy charged that marriage was beyond the workings of the world: "It's about the love. It's not about class. It's not about race. It's not about any of that kind of stuff. It's just about love and two people doing what you should be able to do, and that's love each other." In describing a triumph of love, Addy drew on individualistic meanings for marriage, including its definition as an institution of love.

Addy also valued her marriage for its aid in her own personal growth. In the course of her relationship with Julie, Addy discovered a great deal about herself. This experience further solidified the value of the relationship to her. She explained, "Julie and I come from totally different backgrounds. I grew up in the foster system. And I'm an ex-drug user. I had absolutely no idea what love was, and Julie kind of had to teach me what love was. Through that process I realized that I became a better person by being with her. I think that she completes me in that way." Addy finds access to deeper levels of self-knowledge through her relationship, characterizing the importance and value of relationships insofar as they lead to self-discovery.

In several cases, the association of love with marriage was portrayed as evidence of the similarities between same-sex and different-sex marriage. Contextualizing his marriage to Dale, Pierre, the Canadian citizen, actively paralleled their union to traditional, different-sex marriage: "It's like people saying two guys or two girls getting married is like breaking the notion of marriage. But no, it's the question of love, a question of being together." Pierre and Dale felt strongly about the importance of protecting their ability to be together. Pierre's job sponsors his visa. Should he ever leave his job, he would no longer be able to legally remain in the United States and he would have to leave behind the life he and Dale have together in San Francisco, including the home they own. Like any different-sex couple, Pierre asserted, he and Dale just wanted to be together.

Other respondents emphasized the gravity with which they took their participation in marriage, just as different-sex couples were supposed to. Lois, the physical therapist, insisted, "We took it seriously. It was a serious step. We took it as marriage legally, which is still a very serious step. Financially and everything, you're binding yourself to another human being." But Lois also emphasized that marriage was more than a legal institution and, to be a real marriage, must be supported by personal commitment. Marriage, in other words, was not defined by its institutional meaning. It was made meaningful through the couple's emotions, most specifically love.

Marriage as a symbol of love and commitment was central to Philip's definition of marriage, and he went even farther than Lois in distinguishing the personal commitment aspect from the legal aspect of marriage. As described above, Philip considered his 2003 commitment ceremony to Steven to be his real marriage, not their San Francisco wedding. Philip felt he was married in 2003, even without state sanction. In fact, Philip had no real thoughts about the role of the state in marriage. Explaining why he decided to marry Steven in 2003, Philip said, "We just thought the idea of marriage was something more concrete and more just a thing to do that kind of established our relationship more. . . . It meant more of a commitment to each other, not that we had any sort of open relationship before, but it just was more of a commitment. . . . It was more of a solid commitment versus this is my boyfriend or this is my partner of x amount of years." Marriage was the logical next step in Philip's commitment to Steven, much as marriage is often a rite of passage for heterosexual couples (Cherlin 2004). Together, they planned their ceremony for eight months, invited friends and family, and wrote vows to say to each other.

Having stood up in front of others and committed to Steven, Philip was married, in his mind. No further action was necessary. He said, "In my eyes, we were already married, and I've told Steven this several times. It [legal access to marriage] doesn't matter to me. I know it's a big deal. It's a huge deal for so many people. I just don't let things like that bother me. I see marriages fail all the time and how ridiculous some marriages are. If I had to do it all over again, I would still go to city hall and get married because it was a great experience, but I didn't need it." Philip defined marriage exclusively in cultural terms

regarding how he and Steven created a life together. Legal sanction
was irrelevant. In so doing, he underscored the cultural norms around
marriage as a relationship built on love and commitment, not legal
obligation and the approval of government.

Alan and Chris, among the first couples to receive a marriage
license at city hall, experienced their San Francisco wedding in a similar way: it was simply a legal proceeding. To them, their real marriage
had begun years earlier, following their 2000 commitment ceremony.
Chris explained, "We were already married. If anything, this was kind
of like making it legal." Their existing sense of being married meant
that they did not feel the same urgency about the San Francisco weddings as others. Alan said, "It was amazing to me to see how many
people showed up so fast and how important it was to a lot of people.
I think for us, it was great. But for some people, it seemed very, very
important. For me, it wasn't that important." Alan and Chris so thor-
oughly adopted cultural definitions of marriage grounded in commitment and love that the legal status of the San Francisco weddings was
unimportant to their sense of being married. Rather than suggest that
marriage was not of high value, their lower enthusiasm about their
city hall wedding highlights the way they ascribed an individualistic
meaning to marriage. They defined marriage on their own terms.

As these stories show, some respondents discussed their meanings
for marriage in language that echoed findings on heterosexual meanings for marriage. These narratives of marriage's meaning are common
in popular discourse and lore. Ann Swidler (2001) shows their frequent
manifestation in the lives of heterosexual couples married many years.
These narratives help people to make sense of themselves and their
relationships. They are a cultural resource, whose adoption is not limited to just different-sex couples. Gays and lesbians are members of this
broader culture that values and defines the meaning of marriage, and so
it is unsurprising that some of them voiced these themes of marriage.

Being Treated the Same

Although only a small number of respondents actively characterized
marriage with meanings found commonly among different-sex couples, several nonetheless noted with satisfaction aspects of the wedding
process that underlined their felt equivalence to heterosexual couples.

The marriage process as practiced in San Francisco treated same-sex couples just like different-sex couples in many ways. At the same time, the experience of issuing marriage licenses to same-sex couples made visible ways in which the demand they represent is unique; there are many ways gay and lesbian couples, in the very process of marrying, are not just like straight couples.

The long lines around city hall represent both a similarity and a difference. Ostensibly, all couples interested in marriage licenses, regardless of sexual identity, had to wait in the same line. With the enormously long lines of the first ten days, this was quite a feat. The lines themselves demonstrated that marriage was not just business as usual for lesbian and gay couples. Even with so many respondents describing themselves as already married, these couples came to San Francisco to marry and were willing to wait as long as necessary to do so, even if it took hours or days of waiting. State-sanctioned marriage promised something important and significant enough to persuade couples to wait in line, but it was not assurance of their commitment. The extent of this line shows that same-sex couples are not, strictly speaking, the same as different-sex couples.

On the other hand, once the line had been formed, couples of all sexual identities had to wait in the same line. Steven described seeing straight couples in line on Friday, February thirteenth, as he and Philip waited to marry. He laughed as he remarked that they, for once, "were the minority" and said they were generally good sports about the unexpected line: "I'm sure they've got stories about it, beyond any other city hall couple that's ever been married at city hall. . . . They were generally amused. I think they probably would've just completely rescheduled had they been too upset about it." Here, Steven underscores both the incredible demand for marriage among same-sex couples and the way they were at the mercy of the system. By waiting in line, lesbian and gay couples demonstrated their desire for marriage, but the fact that they could not just hold off on marrying until the lines died down, as straight couples could, evidences the uniqueness of their situation. Further, even as straight couples stood alongside gay and lesbian couples, Steven suspected they received special treatment. He confided, "I think that they probably didn't have to stand in the long line. They were probably a little more whisked through just so that they weren't completely upset by the whole thing." Same-sex marriage seemed different enough from the norm that Steven expected govern-ment workers would make an effort to ensure different-sex couples would be able to avoid the lines and have a "normal" experience. Others saw no hint that straight couples were treated any differently than gay couples. Terrance shared time in line with straight couples wait-ing to get marriage licenses during the appointment period. As described earlier, he initially hesitated about participating in the weddings. Terrance objected to the idea that the state could and would define the terms of his relationship. But once he was there, he appreciated the visual evidence that gay and straight couples were being treated alike:

> Not only were there gay couples who were getting married, but there were heterosexual couples who were getting married. You felt like we were all the same. There wasn't a separation: here are the gay couples [and] here are the straight couples. And the amount of dignity that was given to the whole process, we felt it [and] our friends felt it. The fact that you had to have friends stand for you and had to sign the witness form, you know, brought the sense this is not different than anyone else's experience, which was very nice. It really was one of those times in my life where the joy of the moment was so perfect and that everything slowed down because it was so perfect.

Not all the straight couples appreciated being in the same line as the gay and lesbian couples, however, as Phoebe's experience shows. She related, "I remember standing in line and a male and a female cou-ple came through and the man asked if he could go in front of the line because he wasn't part of this gay marriage thing. And that just perfectly displayed how people look at what same-sex couples do as being something separate or different or odd or strange when all we were trying to do was the same thing that he was trying to do, but he wanted a special line." The straight couple Phoebe witnessed was impatient and insensitive, but did not express overt disapproval of same-sex marriage. As Phoebe notes, their behavior still constituted a form of inequality, albeit without virulent anti-gay rhetoric. As far as Phoebe could discern, this couple was not able to circumvent the line; they had to wait just like any other couple marrying that day.

Once they made it through the line and arrived at the marriage counter, respondents received the exact same treatment as different-sex couples, including receiving a brochure on family planning given to all marrying couples. Same-sex couples were thereby merged into a process designed for different-sex couples, even when parts were not applicable to their situation. Anne, the artist, was highly amused: "And they had to give us this little booklet that was really funny, this straight marriage little booklet, [about] how to get married, with a man and a woman on the front. And we were all cracking up: this is so funny! It was like from the fifties. It's like the standard booklet and you're just like, are you kidding me?" Anne laughed not only at the idea that she and Lynn, the senior center director, needed information about avoiding unwanted pregnancy, but also at its delivery, perceiving its format and content as being outdated. She suggested that straight couples must find the brochure absurd as well. Anne appreciated that she and Lynn received the same content as any other marrying couple and spoke of a shared response to that content that transgressed sexual identity, but the requirement that they receive pregnancy material is nonetheless evidence that getting the "same" treatment is actually getting heteronormative treatment. In Anne and Lynn's experience of receiving the pregnancy information, same-sex couples were presented with the expectation that applicants for marriage licenses are different-sex couples (of reproductive age) and asked to follow the same, albeit unnecessary, procedure.

There were also ways in which the participation of same-sex couples changed the marriage process for different-sex couples. When couples first lined up inside city hall to request marriage licenses, they completed the standard marriage license application. Less than half an hour later, clerks whisked those applications away, causing great anxiety among many participants. As Alan explained, "We were filling [the paperwork] all out and then they realized that it was bride and groom. They had to change the form on the computer, which took a long time, to applicant 1 and applicant 2 'cause those terms are actually copied as your marriage certificate." Since "bride" and "groom" are legal entities, defined as female and male, respectively, city hall employees worried that asking same-sex couples to assign one member to each category would force them to commit perjury and invalidate the licenses immediately. Once the form was rewritten and reprinted, couples could continue with the process. During the weddings and afterward, the city continued the policy of requesting applicant 1 and applicant 2, not bride and groom.

In these ways, gay and lesbian couples' experience of marriage at city hall could be said to be just like straight couples' experience, although the value of such an equivalency is dubious. For instance, same-sex couples (and likely many different-sex couples as well) do not need information on avoiding unwanted pregnancy, rendering no benefit to treating same-sex couples the same as different-sex couples. In the case of the original license fields of "bride" and "groom," however, fitting same-sex couples into a process tailored to different-sex couples is actually problematic, requiring adjustments. Finally, very simply, the existence of the long line of couples is evidence of a pent-up demand for legal marriage that is without parallel among different-sex couples. While perhaps strategically valuable, framing lesbian and gay couples as "the same as" different-sex couples is not entirely accurate.

Ignoring Heteronormativity

Social movement actors have asserted that same-sex couples are just like different-sex couples in their embrace of marriage as an institution grounded in love and commitment. Activists have explicitly mobilized this claim in the campaign for marriage equality, arguing that lesbian and gay couples should be able to marry because they are just like heterosexual couples. In some ways, the evidence provided here bears out these claims. Gay and lesbian couples who married in the 2004 San Francisco weddings often offered meanings in step with contemporary marriage and family findings on the individualistic meanings of marriage. Their statements cite familiar narratives about the meaning and importance of marriage, referencing love, family, and commitment. This use of familiar tropes about marriage is an expected result of a ubiquitous cultural norm about the meaning of marriage (Swidler 2001). Lesbian and gay couples cited love and commitment as meanings for marriage because those are the framings of the institution available in contemporary culture.

Taking these experiences—couples feeling already married and drawing on individualistic meanings for marriage—as evidence that same-sex and different-sex couples are equivalent in their drive to participate in marriage, however, overvalues the effect of this shared culture and erases its heteronormative character. Respondents' stories of the process of applying for a marriage license show how existing assumptions about marriage do not always fit same-sex couples' needs. Moreover, the substantial lines of couples around city hall demonstrate that marriage for gay and lesbian couples is about more than just love and commitment. Although Philip, Alan, and Chris were more casual about their need for the San Francisco wedding license, most of the other respondents—including Philip's partner, Steven—expressed a strong need to participate. Even Terrance, who was initially unsure he wanted to marry, felt very strongly that his marrying mattered, to him, to his family, and to the larger gay and lesbian community.

While the "same as" framing may have strategic value for per-suading elites to support same-sex marriage, it does little to con-test the relationship of heteronormativity and marriage. It does not demand that the institution change to fit the needs of same-sex couples; it does not even suggest that the marriage process might need adjustment to properly accommodate lesbian and gay couples. In fact, much of its claim is premised in the assertion that noth-ing needs to change about marriage because same-sex couples are so similar to different-sex couples. As Bernstein (2001) has shown, a non-confrontational approach may be exactly the recipe for suc-cess in the campaign for marriage equality. Bernstein argues that the legal success of same-sex marriage is dependent on the ability of its advocates to cast it as consistent with, rather than challenging of, heteronormativity. In forwarding an argument of similarity, this is what marriage equality supporters are doing.

However, the consequences of this failure to disrupt heterosexual-ity's normativity include not only preserving heteronormativity but also extending it to same-sex couples. In telling a story where love con-quers all and, more importantly, can remake power relations, there are echoes of the hetero-romantic story of love between men and women (Martin and Kazyak 2009), which, as Wendy Langford (1999) argues, fails to overcome social inequality and instead reproduces unequal power relations between men and women. Given scholars' work on the dangers of narratives of romantic love in obfuscating consumer culture and inequality (Best 2000; Ingraham 1999), claims of similarity in the experience of loving seem unlikely to unmake power relations between heterosexuals and gays and lesbians. Ultimately, denying differences fails to destabilize heteronormativity. Instead, it makes concessions to it, accepting that the heterosexual norm is, in fact, normal.

CHAPTER 5

GENDER AND PARENTHOOD

The men and women who married in the San Francisco weddings engaged with the heteronormative meanings of marriage in different ways. Some used marriage to fiercely contest heteronormativity, while others saw marriage as a way to gain for themselves some of the spoils of normativity—and some did both. Rather than suggest contradiction, these competing understandings should be seen as evidence of heteronormativity's deep social roots. These roots extend into the lives of every member of society, but not always in the same way.

As a social structure, heteronormativity is tied to sexuality—but that's only the beginning. It is implicated in the gender division of labor, distribution of resources, and patriarchal relations of production (Yep 2003). By expecting sexual roles predicated on gender difference, heteronormativity produces the social roles of gender (Ingraham 2005a). Those differences are not value-neutral, and privilege accrues differently to men than to women, to heterosexuals than to homosexuals. Scholars have further argued that heteronormativity is implicated in race (Stokes 2005). Each produces social difference, differentially assigns privilege, and shores up the other's system of privilege. Heteronormativity depends on these differences and reproduces them, reifying systems of privilege.

In essence, heteronormativity constructs distinct social locations, with varying social privilege and power. It follows, then, that the social experience of heteronormativity would be conditioned by social location—and how individuals navigate the heteronormative meanings of marriage would be conditioned by their social location. Same-sex marriage may matter differently to different populations, leading some groups to desire it more than others. Thinking about the possibility that some groups would seek marriage more readily than others, I asked respondents whether they thought there was a typical couple who married in San Francisco. Over and over again, they replied, "No." They insisted that there were couples of all ages, races, and genders. There were families with children and without. There were couples who lived down the street from city hall and couples who flew in from far away. There were couples together for decades and some together less than a year. More than a few respondents explained that there were people of "all shapes and sizes" marrying during the Winter of Love.

Terrance, the retiree, was the first to pop this rosy bubble of limitless diversity among the marrying couples. In response to my question, Terrance briefly tipped his hat to the possibility of being "politically incorrect" and then ventured his impression that more lesbians than gay men married, and more couples with children married. He explained that he didn't mean to stereotype, but that these patterns "just spoke to who really got caught up in this." Kelly, the professor, had a similar feeling that the diversity was not as complete as it might have been. She was suspicious that the population of couples marrying was disproportionately white and upper middle class, largely because they had the social desire to marry. Barbara, the self-described socialist, was attuned to the financial costs of missing work to wait in line, buying food while waiting, and the license itself. Considering these costs, she suggested that the poor would be unlikely to participate in the marriages.

What Terrance, Kelly, and Barbara noticed—or surmised—was that the circumstances of the weddings affected who participated, thereby tacitly acknowledging the importance of social location. Terrance pointed out that the importance of the marriages was different for different couples. Kelly suggested that different segments of the population may feel the imperative to marry differently. And Barbara highlighted how the material circumstances of marrying could pose an obstacle for some. In this chapter, I examine respondents' narratives for the possibility that social location matters in the desire for marriage and for how social location impacted how they navigated the heteronormative character of marriage.

When we dig into respondents' stories with attention to their social identities, we find patterns in how they ascribe meaning to marriage. Their stories reveal the importance of gender, parenthood status, and race in the desire for marriage. Through this social location–inflected investigation, I show that same-sex marriage matters differently to different couples. These differences are best understood through a critical lens that assesses the respective desire for and refusal of heteronormativity's benefits with attention to social location. Respondents' stories highlight the complexity of how individuals assign meaning to (same-sex) marriage, offering purchase on variation in the appeal of heteronormativity. This analysis underscores the complexity of the social structure of heteronormativity and, further, demonstrates its interdependency on other systems of privilege. Such linkages have implications for the success of challenges to heteronormativity.

Gender Matters

I start with an investigation into how gender mattered in the San Francisco weddings. As it turns out, the San Francisco marriages were characterized by a demographic puzzle: more lesbians married than gay men (57 percent to 43 percent). Lest we underrate this gender imbalance, according to the 2000 census, there are more male same-sex-coupled households than female same-sex-coupled households in the United States (Simmons and O'Connell 2003). Nationwide, one in nine unmarried, coupled households in the 2000 census contained same-sex partners, with the roughly 301,000 gay couples (51 percent of same-sex, unmarried, coupled households) outnumbering their approximately 293,000 lesbian counterparts. California, where 91 percent of the same-sex couples married in 2004 hailed from (Teng 2004), had the highest number of same-sex-coupled households, representing about 16 percent of the national total and 1.4 percent (N = 92,138) of the total of California households. In California, as was the case at the national level, male-partnered households (54 percent) outnumbered female households (46 percent).

This higher rate of lesbian marriages becomes particularly salient in light of these overall lower numbers in the population. Although same-sex marriage is framed in a gender-neutral way and advocates frame it as important to all queer people, the gender imbalance among participants in San Francisco suggests that among these two groups—gay men and lesbians—there is an inaccurate assumption of equal stakes in, equal demand for, and equal benefit from access to same-sex marriage. Understanding the meanings and experiences of same-sex marriage requires attention to gender.

This trend of higher lesbian participation has continued as same-sex marriage has become legal in states across the nation, with lesbian couples outnumbering gay men couples nearly two to one (Badgett and Herman 2011). Popular theory holds that more women than men married because of women's greater desire—whether innate or socially constructed—for marriage. News articles depicting two brides in white dresses have referenced cultural lore of men's reluctance to marry and women's deep desire for it, mobilizing quintessential heteronormative tropes to suggest that gender is the explanatory variable when it comes to the high rate of lesbian marriage.

There is certainly a substantial literature identifying the complex gender pressures enacted in (different-sex) weddings (Geller 2001; Howard 2006; Otnes and Pleck 2003) and even evidence that weddings themselves produce normative gender (Ingraham 1999). However, I do not find evidence in my sample that women were more likely to invoke a deep desire for contemporary marriage than men. Men talked about marriage in line with its contemporary meaning the same way that women did. Looking at the numbers, 38 percent (N = 9) of the women I interviewed offered individualistic meanings for marriage, as did 33 percent (N = 6) of the men I interviewed. Throwing around percentages and raw numbers in a qualitative study is always problematic, of course, but I offer these figures as support for my qualitative analysis, finding no difference between men and women in their assignment of the normative love and commitment meanings for marriage.

In contrast, men and women talked about the other three meanings for marriage—as a political statement, as a means to secure legal rights, and as a means to gain social recognition—in qualitatively different ways. On the political front, women were more likely to express ambivalence about their participation, wanting to support the cause but suspicious of the institution of marriage, pointing to marriage's history of exacerbating inequality rather than ameliorating it. They wanted to show solidarity with other lesbians and gay men and embrace an opportunity to expose heterosexual privilege, but they had reservations about marriage. Ultimately, because the San Francisco weddings were *same-sex* weddings, they joined in, drawing a distinction between marriage and same-sex marriage. The latter, they asserted, could be used for political ends to remake heterosexual privilege.

There were differences between men and women in their use of legal and social meanings as well. Men tended to be interested in different legal rights than women, with men citing hospital visitation and rights of partner inheritance while women more frequently talked about parental rights afforded through marriage. There was, in other words, a notable divergence between the legal concerns men described desiring and the legal benefits women sought. In their use of social meanings as well, women referenced children and family while men did not. George Chauncey (2004) has suggested that both the AIDS crisis and the rise of lesbian and gay parenthood contributed to the demand for marriage in San Francisco. Here, I apply a gendered lens to this argument: the AIDS crisis predominantly took the lives of gay men, and lesbians are much more likely to be parents. I offer evidence of how the gendered experience of these two occurrences impacts lesbians' and gay men's understandings of same-sex marriage and argue that this difference can be generalized to same-sex marriage experiences beyond San Francisco.

By looking beyond generic assumptions of women's emotional need for marriage to empirically interrogate how lesbians' stories of their San Francisco weddings differed from gay men's, we see that the politicized environment—the opportunity to contest heteronormativity—influenced lesbians' participation in San Francisco. Such study also demonstrates the hegemony of the belief that marriage marks a family. The persistent link between family and marriage does not bode well for same-sex marriage's potential to disrupt the relationship between marriage and heteronormativity.

Ambivalence about Marriage

Just moments into our interview, Cynthia, the federal employee, explained, "I don't believe in the institution of marriage." I was confused. Cynthia and Janet had waited in line for six hours to marry. This behavior did not seem to fit with Cynthia's professed lack of interest in marriage. Talking with Janet, the nurse, did not clear up my confusion either. She, too, had little interest in marriage as an institution. As the interview continued, I came to understand Cynthia's ambivalence as a negotiation of how change can happen. She wanted to see dramatic changes to the social order, but making them seemed to require her to participate in parts of the very order she wanted to undo.

Cynthia saw marriage as a deeply heteronormative institution. She didn't trust it. Like her, six other women respondents also described their suspicion of marriage. They spoke of distrust for marriage, often owing to marriage's history as a patriarchal institution and the larger question of its utility for organizing society. Marriage was not the capstone of a relationship, essential for a civilized society, or even a best practice for all individuals and relationships. Through personal experience and exposure to feminist thinking, these women were not sold on marriage.

In identifying the heteronormative aspects of marriage, however, these respondents also actively engaged in the question of whether *same-sex* marriage could disrupt those aspects. Torn between a critique of the institution and a desire to support lesbian and gay rights, respondents in this subset were conflicted about marrying.

An initial reason for some respondents' wariness of marriage came from childhood experiences. Elizabeth, the accounting assistant, compared marriage to incarceration: "It meant prison [laughs]. I decided in third grade I wasn't getting married because I didn't want to share my checkbook with anybody. I saw my parents fight over money, and I thought, 'I'm not doing that.' So I had it pretty well set in my mind from a young age that marriage was not in the cards." Sophie, the graduate student, also had a history of distrust of marriage, owing to her mother's experience and that of her peers' parents when she was growing up. She said, "I didn't have a good experience with marriage from being a kid in a family. My parents divorced when I was three. My mom married again and had an abusive second husband. I was raised in a generation where most of my friends' parents divorced, so it didn't seem to be a sustaining institution for a lot of people. I remember the button that said marriage is a great institution if you like being institutionalized [laughs]. I had periods of my life where I was kind of along that vein."

As they grew up, these early experiences were brought into focus and these women saw marriage—and divorce—not just as a personal pitfall but as systematically problematic. They saw flaws in the institution itself, not just as a binding commitment but, more specifically, in how it controls women (Finlay and Clarke 2003). Dating from the 1970s, feminists have argued that marriage is an institution fundamentally about constraint—or even colonization (Hagan 1993)—that denies women sexual freedom through mandatory monogamy (Robinson 1997; Rosa 1994; Stelboum 1999), grants men sexual access to women (Jaggar 1994), and allows men to profit from women's labor, both in and outside of the home (Bunch 1987). These arguments continue, as Rosemary Auchmuty (2004, 105) argues: "200 years of feminist agreement that marriage permits, even encourages, oppression makes the institution untouchable and irredeemable in the eyes of many women, including myself. For many feminists today, revulsion against it is so engrained it feels instinctive. Others who have chosen to marry do so with an awareness that the gesture is in part a compromise and that they will have to struggle against a set of normative assumptions they themselves reject." These criticisms of the institution of marriage have frequently encompassed criticisms of heterosexuality more broadly (Bunch 1987; Rich 1980; Richardson 1996).

Respondents echoed these critiques and characterized marriage as "antiquated" and "useless." Many described it as having a history of oppressing women. Susan, a forty-nine-year-old librarian, said, "I think it's a really sort of antiquated institution that hasn't served women well over the years and throughout history." Sonia, the public employee, made a similar point, saying, "[Marriage] was a made-up institution primarily for—my opinion—the benefit of men. . . . A lot of the laws were set up to keep women in their place. If a woman decided to get a divorce and she had a joint checking account, credit cards jointly, all her credit tied into the man, then when she gets a divorce, what's she got? Zilch. That's just crazy. I think it [marriage] was thought up by a woman, but I think men exploited it. Given those dynamics, no, I wasn't going to give a man that legal control over me, no! Uh-uh. I just couldn't see doing it." Susan and Sonia explained that they were wary of marriage and always expected that they would opt out of it.

Others went further, questioning the utility of marriage as an organizing institution at all—echoing feminist calls for the abolition of marriage (Auchmuty 2004)—and challenging the prerogative of the state to sanction relationships and dole out benefits accordingly. Sophie, the graduate student, explained, "I really believe in universal healthcare and actually don't think that only married people should have the benefits that married people get." Barbara, a socialist, explained that, to her, "marriage itself is a feature of capitalism. It's a feature of the state. It's a bourgeois institution. It's a way of getting the state away from actually providing the benefits to individuals. In the real world, even in a capitalist world, individuals deserve certain things. What should their marital status have to do with anything? Why should being married get you health benefits or anything else? So generally I'm opposed to the concept of marriage." For Barbara, it was not just that marriage wasn't for her, she objected to marriage's entire existence.

In particular, respondents critiqued marriage for building a division between the married and the unmarried, for differently valuing their status, and for allowing the state to be the arbiter of romantic relationships. Barbara said, "I think of it as an institution of capitalism that denies benefits to non-married people. And also it has a way of instituting state control into people's private lives." Barbara's concerns have been fleshed out by scholars. Mary Hunt (2003) argues that same-sex marriage will encourage the extension of a dichotomy of unequal social worth and value between the married and the unmarried, one with differential disadvantages for men and women, into the lesbian and gay community.

Finally, some respondents questioned the liberatory potential of marriage because it is what straight people do, not queer people. Sophie saw marriage as about civil and human rights, but not as something that would transform the role of lesbian and gay people in society. Indeed, her concern about its purported leveling effects made her less sanguine about gaining access to legal marriage: "I didn't necessarily think [same-sex] marriage was a radical thing. And I still think that that's up for grabs in some ways. I think that there's a very conservative element of our [the lesbian and gay] community that really grabs onto marriage as an institution to sort of have us be like everybody else. I'm not really all about that. I don't think that diversity and social change happen by everybody being just like each other. It's not my goal. I like salads [and] I like soups. I love the way that we connect across and through and with different-ness. I had mixed feelings about [marrying]." Yet despite respondents' characterization of marriage as something saturated with heterosexuality, they desired marriage, as Sophie alludes to in her reference to "mixed feelings." These conflicting feelings illustrate the complicated position advocates for gays and lesbians find themselves in. Simply put, these respondents were ambivalent about marriage. Much the same way lesbian mothers have described mixed feelings about assuming the traditional life-course trappings of heterosexual women by opting in to motherhood (Mezey 2008), they wondered: could they make their own meanings for marriage?

Overcoming Ambivalence

In the end, they decided they could. As Kath Weston (1991) argues of gays and lesbians in the 1980s discovering that they could make their own rules about family formation, these seven women participated in the San Francisco weddings despite their ambivalence about marriage as an institution. They did so largely by distinguishing marriage from *same-sex* marriage. Kelly, the professor, for example, explained that she and Michelle wanted to get married to unmake some of the anti-feminist meanings of marriage: "[Marriage is] a patriarchal institution that we were excluded from. So the irony, of course, is that we wanted in to that institution—to transform it from the inside." Given the extensive literature finding same-sex households to be more egalitarian than different-sex households (Blumstein and Schwartz 1983; Chan et al. 1998; Kurdek 1993, 1995; Patterson et al. 2004; Solomon et al. 2004), we might expect Kelly's hope to come to fruition. Same-sex households have been shown to undo some of the gendered expectations about how households run, and it follows that same-sex marriage might similarly undo some of the patriarchal meanings of marriage.

Sonia surprised herself in discovering that all the reasons she would never marry a man were the reasons she wanted to marry her partner. Implicit in her response is her awareness of her same-sex relationship as less socially secure, perhaps because of generalized social condemnation (Auchmuty 2004), than an analogous different-sex relationship. She said, "I felt like all the reasons that I wouldn't marry a man are the reasons that I decided to marry a woman. Again, the feeling of security was important, whereas, with a man, that was never important. I guess in some ways, it kind of made me do a [reversal] because I didn't believe in marriage, but I didn't hesitate when the opportunity came up." In balancing their suspicion of marriage with their desire to forward lesbian and gay rights, Kelly and Sonia emphasized the difference between marriage and same-sex marriage. Some of that difference would come from its participants' gender alone, and some would come from marrying couples' active work for change.

Barbara, the socialist, and her partner, Gayle, went to city hall to marry as well. Despite their political beliefs about the capitalist nature of marriage, they waited in line for a total of fifteen hours over two days to marry. In describing the experience, Barbara touched on both the liberatory potential of same-sex marriage and its problematic institutional consequences, saying, "The positive political significance is I feel like I did participate in a movement that was trying to change society's attitudes about homosexuality, more than anything else—to say that you can't deny lesbians and gay men the rights that you grant to everyone else. And that was good. In a negative way, my participation meant that I helped kind of prop up the institution of marriage, which denies those same benefits to non-coupled people." As Barbara's explanation evidences, not all respondents found it easy to distinguish marriage from same-sex marriage. Barbara worried that the history of marriage would carry through to same-sex couples who participated in the institution.

Marrying in San Francisco did not change Barbara's beliefs about marriage. She still considers it an institution of capitalism and challenges its central role in society. But in 2004, she also saw the possibility of showing solidarity and standing up for gay and lesbian rights through marriage. Like the other six women who expressed ambivalence about marriage as an institution, Barbara had to negotiate political beliefs that came into conflict in that instant: support for lesbian and gay rights and a critique of marriage. She had to decide whether she believed that by marrying she could contest heterosexual privilege. All seven reported feeling pulled in multiple directions: desiring to advocate for gay and lesbian equal rights but cautious about the patriarchal history of marriage; cognizant of the negative institutional meanings of marriage, including the acceptance of the state as an arbiter of romantic relationships (Butler 2002), but enticed by the possibility that *same-sex* marriage could unmake heteronormativity. In their narratives of the events, they took on heteronormativity explicitly, calling for a broader revision of the practice of marriage itself.

The historical overlaps between lesbianism and feminism are well documented (Echols 1989; Stein 1997; Taylor and Rupp 2005; Taylor and Whittier 1992), suggesting that the fact that all of the respondents who voiced hesitation about marriage as an institution were women is not an accident. This is not to say that only lesbians are attuned to heteronormativity; gay men in my sample also offered pointed critiques of heteronormativity. Nevertheless, I find that individuals with exposure to a feminist critique of marriage—more often lesbians than gay men—are more likely to be attuned to how heteronormativity is (re)produced *through* the institution of marriage. That is, they are more likely to understand marriage as a heteronormative institution. Gay men and lesbians without exposure to the feminist critique of marriage are less likely to view marriage this way, but certainly may have a heightened awareness of other institutions and practices that perpetuate heteronormativity. To the extent that same-sex marriage is a protest tactic of the lesbian and gay rights movement, as my colleagues and I have argued elsewhere (Taylor et al. 2009), women who embrace a feminist critique of marriage may see marrying as an important act of protest and be more likely to wed.

Family Matters

While attunement to the political contestation possibilities of same-sex marriage may encourage lesbians to marry, a second way to understand the gender gap focuses on how the normative benefits of marriage may operate as an incentive for lesbians to wed. Men and women did not talk about the normative benefits—the legal and social meanings of marriage—in the same ways. Despite the apparent across-the-board marriage benefit of legal rights, men highlighted different rights than women. For example, men more frequently mentioned legal benefits related to hospitalization and dying that would protect one partner in the event of the other's death. Ernesto said marriage is "the legal protection that you need if someone's sick." He elaborated, "We've been together for many years, and we've seen people that have encountered some real, real bad situations from family and things like that because they did not have the strength of the legal document that said: 'These people belong together. What belongs to one, belongs to the other.'" Jeffrey, the retired physician, related the story of how the family of his previous partner contested his will after he died of AIDS. From that experience, Jeffrey was sensitized to the protections of legal marriage. Frank's life, too, was entirely up-ended when Henry, his partner of fifty years, died. When Henry passed away, Frank found himself nearly destitute, unable to access Henry's social security benefits or pension and, at seventy years old, unable to generate an income for himself. Thanks to a generous friend, Frank was given a place to sleep, but otherwise would have been homeless.

The articulated concern over the legal implications for a surviving partner makes sense given the devastating history of AIDS in the gay community. As Chauncey (2004) argues, not only did HIV and AIDS cause a spike in deaths of gay men during the 1980s and 1990s, the disease brought the gay community into contact with a medical and legal system that was often highly homophobic. Partners were routinely excluded from visiting their loved ones in hospitals; stories abounded of legal preference being given to families with which a man had little contact over his surviving, committed partner. These experiences, and stories about them, likely attuned the gay community to the importance of the legal protections of marriage.

While some women did cite legal meanings for marriage associated with concern over hospitalization and dying—notably, Sandra, who suffered from a degenerative disease and worried where her illness would leave Olivia, her partner of six years—most of the legal meanings women offered drew on concerns about parental rights, including second-parent adoption and inheritance for their children. Noting that eleven of the twelve parents in my sample were women offers important context for this gender disparity. Indeed, the popularity of parenthood-related legal concerns among women may owe less to gender and more to parenthood status. The apparent gender gap may be better understood as a parenthood gap.

The Parenthood Effect

As figure 5.1 shows, parents were noticeably less likely to offer an individualistic meaning for marriage than were respondents without children. Childfree respondents offered individualistic meanings for marriage at a startlingly higher rate than respondents with children: while 41 percent of childfree respondents gave individualistic meanings for marriage, only 23 percent of parents did (fig. 5.1). These childfree respondents talked about marriage in terms of their relationship to their spouse. The handful of parents who gave individualistic meanings for marriage, however, often referenced their children. Michelle, for example, explained that she married Kelly for love, commitment, and to give their two-year-old son a legally recognized family. Overall, parents infrequently offered individualistic meanings for marriage, suggesting that such personal meanings are less important to parents than to childfree respondents.

Figure 5.1 further shows that respondents with children were more likely to cite a social meaning for marriage than childfree respondents. Parents invoked social meanings for marriage 67 percent of the time, whereas respondents without children cited such meanings only 48 percent of the time. Clearly, social meanings for marriage are

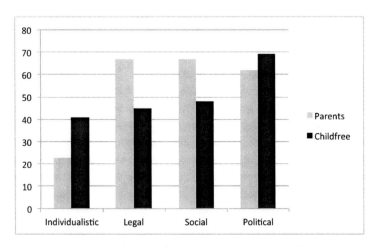

Figure 5.1 Percentage of Respondents Citing Four Meanings of Marriage, by Parenthood

more important to parents than non-parents. In addition, the higher rate of social meanings is coupled with a higher rate of legal meanings by parents: 67 percent of parents offered legal meanings for marriage, compared to just 45 percent of childfree respondents.

The importance of legal rights for respondents with children is clear from the interviews with parents. As Deirdre, mother of two children, said, "Our relationship isn't missing anything, but our family's legal stability is." Deirdre commented on the legal benefits of marriage, including rights of inheritance and ease of second-parent adoption in particular. Both of these things are notably easier to establish for married couples. Kelly, mother of one child, explained that marriage would have made the process of building their family easier. She said, "I just felt like we had spent thousands and thousands of dollars to try to approximate marriage to protect our son, to come as close to it as possible. We had to go through the whole process of having a social worker come to our home and visit to make sure that we would both have legal rights to him [as mandated by the law]. I was the biological mother, but we don't make that distinction, but we knew the law would." Marriage would have saved Kelly and Michelle from needing state approval to legally establish their family. Kelly said, "It just felt like, to me, marriage was something that would've allowed us to avoid all that, save thousands of dollars, and save the humiliation of having a social worker judge us as a family. We were so thrilled when the judge granted Michelle the second-parent adoption and we were celebrating and very happy. We both cried. But at the same time, it's so angering." Completing the second-parent adoption was a happy milestone, but Kelly nonetheless recognized that it was a milestone married different-sex couples get to avoid.

In some cases, the encouragement toward marriage came from the children themselves. Diana and Mia, together for eight years at the time, were returning to their Northern California home when the weddings began, after being out of town for several days. En route, Diana called her seventeen-year-old daughter to let her know they were on their way home. Her daughter told her to turn around and head into San Francisco to get married and make their family official. After many hours in line, Diana and Mia were married, with Diana's daughter there by phone. As she described it, "We just had her on the cell phone and had her listening to the ceremony. And they pronounced us married. I get back on the phone to listen to my daughter, see if she heard all of it, and all I could do was hear her crying because she was so happy she was there with us." Diana identified her daughter's insistence as the causal force in her and Mia's decision to marry. In this light, we could say that Diana and Mia married *because* they were parents.

Children were an impetus for Isabel's decision to marry as well. She explained that legal protections mattered, but so did social recognition as a family: "We're [gays and lesbians are] in every state, according to the census, and we're not going anywhere. And there's a lot of rights that our kids don't have because we're not seen as legitimate couples. And that's not fair to the kids. Just civil rights is not enough. Marriage is the only way we're going to be seen as equal citizens." In part, Isabel was marrying for the kids.

These statements from parents tell us that social definitions of family are tightly linked to marriage, especially when children are involved. And quite explicitly, marriage matters both legally and socially. By sanctioning specific relationships as protected under the law and associating them with particular rights and responsibilities, the state plays a key role in the determination and formation of the naturalized social construct of "the family." Parents are uniquely primed to the legal protections and social legitimacy that come with marriage. Scholarship on gay and lesbian family formation helps to explain this, offering evidence of the unique positionality of these families (Badgett 2009; Lewin 1993; Mamo 2007; Mezey 2008; M. Sullivan 2004). In particular, scholars have noted the complicated interactions gay and lesbian families must experience legally (Dalton 2001) and socially (Lewin 1993) to be seen as legitimate families. M. V. Lee Badgett (2001) argues that gay and lesbian parents are at a particular disadvantage in the law since the law assumes each child has exactly one mother and one father. In effect, they have to have an encounter with the system in order to be parents.

This makes the legal rights of gay and lesbian parents particularly precarious and may operate as a disincentive to them entering parenthood. While gay men and lesbians may desire children at the same rate as heterosexuals (Weston 1991), social and legal challenges may conspire to reduce the rate at which gays and lesbians become parents.

On the social front, lesbian and gay parents experience a complex set of identifications since mainstream society equates homosexuality with the lack of a family. As gays and lesbians and their children struggle to assert the validity of their chosen families and expand the notion of kinship, heteronormative assumptions about parenthood are pointedly felt (Weston 1991) and the power of the state in conferring legitimacy on a family is made manifest.

The meanings cited by currently childfree respondents who plan to have children in the future underscore that these associations of legal and social import with marriage among parents likely stem from the actual experience of parenthood, rather than the desire for children. Two women in the sample said they planned to have children, and two men said they might have children in the future. Although it is tricky to draw conclusions from this small set of respondents, I note that only one of the four invoked a legal meaning for marriage and just two of the four cited a social meaning for wedding. The lower frequencies of both legal and social meanings for marriage among these two couples, compared to parents, suggest that there is a difference between the desire for children and the experience of having children. This is consistent with work on the impact of parenthood on heterosexuals. In his study of the emergence of adulthood among heterosexual men and women, Jeffrey Arnett (2004) finds that the experience of becoming a parent is catalyzing in the life course. Parents reported qualitatively different experiences of adulthood than non-parents and, moreover, than non-parents predicted would matter. There is evidence, in other words, that the experience of parenthood changes one's outlook in unanticipated ways, highlighting the importance, perhaps, of the social and legal aspects of marriage.

A final comparison is instructive. There were two couples in my sample in which one of the members identified as transgender. Both were eligible to have their sex of record formally changed on state paperwork. What that meant is that the couple would now be different-sex, legally speaking, and permitted to marry in the state of California. For Laura and Elizabeth, this opportunity was not one they planned to capitalize on. Laura explained, "To me, that's more of a cop-out thing, because I'm no different. I'm not a different person than I was when they said it was illegal. It's just that now I can meet some legal standard that says that I can have male ID. But I don't really look any different or anything than I did before. It feels like it would be an affront to every other gay person who can't and wants to." Despite their ability to get their relationship legally recognized once Laura legally changed her sex, neither wanted to marry until same-sex marriage became legal. Their firm sense of queer identity precluded them from leveraging a loophole, of sorts, that would allow them legal recognition.

Phoebe and Alex planned to take a different route. Soon after my interview with Phoebe, Alex was going to complete the paperwork to be legally recognized as male. The two were very excited. Phoebe explained, "There're two schools of thought right now. We're either going to just run out the minute we have the court order on December twelfth and get married. Or we're going to wait until our actual anniversary on the thirty-first and get married then, in October. One, of course, being more sentimental. The other, of course, being just to make sure that all of our protections are in place." In her comment, Phoebe underscores the importance of legal protections for her and Alex. Unlike Laura and Elizabeth, Phoebe and Alex have a daughter. Although Phoebe expressed conflicted feelings about taking advantage of marriage when other couples could not, she was very clear that marriage was important because of their daughter: "We want to make sure that our property goes to our daughter."

The Continuing Importance of Gender

The persistent association of marriage with family also offers insight into the gender gap in participation in the San Francisco weddings: in the California population, lesbians are far more likely to be parents than gay men (Simmons and O'Connell 2003). In California, 34.4 percent of lesbian same-sex-coupled households in the 2000 census had children under eighteen, compared to just 20.2 percent of gay men same-sex-coupled households and compared to 50.9 percent of different-sex, married, coupled households (Simmons and O'Connell 2003). I suggest here that women's higher frequency of parenthood is a biographical feature that makes them more likely to cite social and legal meanings for marriage and, in turn, be mobilized to marry.

Scholars have explicitly analyzed the rise of lesbian motherhood (Lewin 1993; Mamo 2007; Mezey 2008) and the parallel lack of a rise in gay fatherhood, arguing that its emergence owes partly to the ease of accomplishment—many lesbians can become pregnant themselves with

the aid of a sperm donor; gay men must rely on at least one other body—
and partly to social conditions, including the belief that a child a woman
bears can be solely hers to parent. Research demonstrates that this gap in
parenting rates is not the product of lesbians wanting children at higher
rates than gay men (Gates et al. 2007). Citing the rise of the lesbian
and gay rights movement, the increasing visibility of lesbian mothers,
the rise of reproductive and conceptive technologies, and the women's
movement—or, more specifically, the women's health movement—
scholars have described the emergent phenomenon of lesbian motherhood as the lesbian baby boom, or "gayby" boom (Chauncey 2004; Mamo
2007; Mezey 2008). To this list of catalyzing factors, scholars have also
added the HIV/AIDS epidemic and its encouragement of a celebration of
life in the gay community (Mezey 2008; Weston 1991).

While lesbians had these various factors encouraging and enabling
them to become parents, not to mention their biological availability, gay
men were in a very different situation. Scholars have found gay men as
interested in parenthood as lesbians (Weston 1991), but their inability
to literally carry their own children (McKinney 1987) and their frequent
exclusion from adoption because of homophobic laws (Infanti 2007) significantly impact their ability to achieve parenthood. In Nancy Mezey's
(2008) terminology, they had the desire but structural constraints pre-
vented the realization of that desire. The rise of AIDS compounded the
difficulty gay men had in becoming parents, virtually eliminating the
formation of three-parent (or more) families, such as a lesbian couple
and their gay male friend. Fearing the rate of HIV infection among gay
men, lesbians in the 1980s increasingly turned to sperm banks and anonymous donors, where they had formerly asked gay male friends to donate
and potentially share parenting responsibilities (Weston 1991). Currently,
sperm banks routinely refuse gay men as sperm donors, conflating sexual
identity with HIV risk, thus reducing the ability of gay men to even anon-
ymously father children (Mamo 2007). Together, these features form the
foundation of the parenthood gap in the gay and lesbian community seen
in population numbers today (Mezey 2008; Weston 1991).

There is some reason to believe that even if men and women
reached parity in parenthood, lesbian mothers would continue to
be more interested in marriage than their counterparts. The experience of achieving pregnancy and negotiating familial status and

rights affects women in qualitatively different ways as they are constructed into the identity of patient (Mamo 2007) or mother (with presumed heterosexuality, see Lewin 1993). For example, lesbians who choose insemination undergo a different process to achieve parenthood, complete with attendant discursive constructions, than gay men. Despite insemination for lesbians being technically equivalent to the practice of inseminating heterosexual women, the medical discourse and institutional procedures surrounding the use of these technologies formally accommodates only the latter, with the former somewhat awkwardly fit into existing categories required not by the technology but by the social apparatuses that surround it (J. Murphy 2001). For instance, lesbians commonly must be diagnosed as "infertile" to qualify for reproductive technologies, thereby conforming to standards designed to diagnose heterosexual couples.

Further, lesbian motherhood, in general, entails a unique set of legal challenges (Mezey 2008), including the intricacies of what Laura Mamo (2007) terms "achieving pregnancy," such as negotiating the rights of the donor and the medicalization of pregnancy. Legal marriage would eliminate the legal loopholes lesbians face, for instance, in using donated sperm since the law currently legislates parental rights based on marital ties (Mamo 2007). The same complexities do not confront gay men who become parents (although certainly a different set of legal challenges accompany gay men's achievement of parenthood).

Socially, too, lesbian mothers are in a unique position. Ellen Lewin (1993) has shown that lesbian mothers frequently experience an erasure of their sexual identity as strangers presume motherhood requires heterosexuality. To the extent that lesbians' sexual identity is erased by parenthood, lesbian mothers may be particularly interested in marriage as a means of publicly establishing their lesbian identity, and we may continue to find that lesbians and gay men have different meanings and uses for marriage.

Race and Class Matters

Just as gender and parenthood status mattered in how respondents thought through their participation in marriage, my interviews offer some support for the importance of race as well. Eleven of the respondents I interviewed were people of color (five men and six women; 26 percent of the sample). They offered individualistic, legal, and political meanings for marriage roughly in line with their white counterparts, but far fewer invoked social meanings for marriage (fig. 5.2). Specifically, only three of the respondents of color discussed marriage in terms of its ability to confer cultural legitimacy or social recognition. They constituted just 27 percent of the respondents of color, in contrast to 65 percent (N = 20) of the white respondents who cited a social meaning of marriage.

In essence, respondents of color were much less likely than white respondents to frame marriage in terms of its social meaning. Whereas white respondents often saw marriage as a path to establishing themselves as a family in the eyes of others, respondents of color did not generally see marriage that way. This points to an underlying pattern of race in how respondents thought about marriage as a social institution. Indeed, the predominance of white respondents offering meanings for marriage that cited its ability to confer family status suggests that the association of marriage with family is mediated not only by heteronormativity but also by whiteness. Nonwhite respondents did not invoke marriage as a primary means to signal to others their status as a family, which may be consistent with alternative understandings of kinship in some communities (Cherlin 2009).

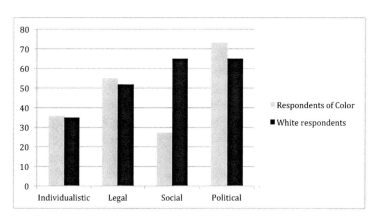

Figure 5.2 Percentage of Respondents Citing Four Meanings of Marriage, by Race

This association of heteronormativity and race should not come as a surprise—sexuality has long been used to perpetuate systems of race (Collins 2005)—but most conversations about heteronormativity focus on sexual identity and gender. Mason Stokes (2005) is one of the few scholars to explore the relationships between heterosexuality and whiteness, positing that they operate as "normative copartners." He argues that heteronormativity and race collaboratively produce privileged and marginalized identities. When white respondents spoke of mobilizing marriage to achieve some of its normative social benefits, in effect, they were not just seeking the spoils of normativity; they were also leveraging race privilege.

Melanie Heath (2009) has framed marriage as privileging not only specific sexual and racial identities, but also social class. She argues that marriage has been constructed as heterosexual, white, and middle class, particularly when it comes to the ideal family it is supposed to describe. The normative family that marriage aims to produce, in other words, is not only one of different-sex partners, but one whose members are white and middle class. Given these findings, it is not hard to imagine that class, too, matters to the practice of same-sex marriage and the navigation of heteronormativity. Likely due to the predominance of relatively affluent respondents (income over $75,000; N = 29; 69 percent) and the near absence of respondents representing lower-income strata (only one respondent reported an income below $35,000; only two respondents fell into the $35,000–74,000 category) in my sample, however, these data cannot speak to variation in the appeal of heteronormativity by class.

Although same-sex couples are outside of the normative expectations of marriage, those whose only deviation from that norm is in their sexual identity may identify more closely with the norm, experiencing both greater desire for and greater access to the spoils of normativity. Thus, not only does the push for same-sex marriage as a means to gain normative status preserve the association of marriage with family, it may unintentionally reify the ways normativity privileges whiteness and middle-class status.

Remaking Marriage?

Although respondents from different social locations alike talked about marriage in ways that highlighted its political, legal, and social meanings, there are nonetheless distinctions in their use. Several women—and no men—grappled with marriage's history as a patriarchal institution. They saw it as a heterosexual practice and, as such, had no interest in marriage. But when city hall began issuing marriage licenses, they wondered, is *same-sex* marriage different? For them, same-sex marriage offered a unique way to make a political statement contesting heteronormativity. Going forward, we can imagine that other lesbians drawing on a feminist critique of marriage may similarly see marriage as an opportunity to challenge heterosexual privilege and be inspired to marry.

Parents, too, showed heightened interest in marrying in San Francisco. Their drive for marriage points to the ways in which the family as a construct is firmly undergirded by the dominant culture's definition of what is normative and, in turn, defines what is considered normal (Bourdieu 1998). Even as marriage's meaning has changed over time, it is closely associated with definitions of family in contemporary America (Powell et al. 2010). The experience of being recognized by others as a family according to one's own self-definition is immensely appealing (Connell 2009), and these data show that many respondents got caught up in the legal and social spoils of being recognized as a normative family. As couples with children take advantage of the social and legal benefits of state-sanctioned marriage, their participation has clear benefits to them as a family unit. It also tacitly reifies the association of marriage with children and a definition of family premised on two parents. The question of same-sex marriage is not just about who is defined as a legitimate married couple, but what constitutes a (legitimate) family.

The brief discussion of variation by race and class rounds out our thinking about how difference in social location matters in the practice of same-sex marriage. White respondents more often drew on social meanings for marriage that preserve the benefits of normative status than did respondents of color, pointing to ways in which normativity is tied to whiteness. This suggests that reifying heteronormativity matters to a range of marginalized social locations, not just gays and lesbians. There may not have been a typical couple at the weddings, but there is evidence of marriage's continued use to perpetuate privilege.

CHAPTER 6

THE PERSISTENT POWER
OF MARRIAGE

The preceding chapters have largely focused on respondents' narratives of navigating heteronormative associations, examining how same-sex couples contest or strategically mobilize aspects of heteronormativity through marriage. Heteronormativity, however, is not solely constituted by practice; it also determines practice. The institution of marriage, even if its heteronormative underpinnings are challenged, is likely to have significant impacts on the lives of lesbians and gays. In this chapter, I examine three ways the institution of marriage changes the lives of same-sex couples. I begin by looking at individual relationships. Although the men and women I interviewed had been together for many years when they married, some of them reported that marriage actually changed their relationship. To their great surprise, some respondents felt different after they were married—more committed and more connected to their partner. Their experiences illustrate the normative power of the institution to orient the behavior of its participants: we have ideas about how married couples are supposed to behave and, regardless of how they interacted prior to their San Francisco wedding, some respondents felt the weight of those expectations after their ceremonies.

Of course, many more respondents insisted that marriage did not change their relationship, but they experienced the normative power of marriage in other ways. Marriage, as a status, orients the behavior of others. It comes with a set of social expectations about how people outside the marriage, both familiars and strangers, should treat the couple. Some respondents actively leveraged these social conventions, demanding that others treat their partner as they would a different-sex spouse. Others found themselves on the receiving end of changed behavior without making any effort. Across my interviews, I heard stories from respondents about how their newly acquired status as married compelled a cascade of changes in their everyday lives. The emergence of these apparent spoils of normativity absent respondents' intent demonstrates the potency of marital status to cue the legitimacy of family relationships, and thus the deep connection between heteronormativity and marriage. Marriage itself does not necessarily change these couples (and their families), but it does change the way both the law and society interact with them.

In orienting behavior, both within and with these marriages, marrying introduced new scripts into respondents' lives. Legal same-sex marriage also holds the possibility of displacing existing scripts, particularly those used to celebrate commitment. Research on commitment ceremonies shows that many same-sex couples already borrow heavily from the familiar wedding script of one couple, an official, and a gathering of family and friends (Hull 2006; Lewin 1998). However, among my respondents, I also find evidence of rich diversity in commitment scripts, including no formal commitment ceremony and ceremonies that take place exclusively between the two members of the couple. With access to legal marriage, it is unlikely that many of these scripts will continue to feel legitimate. State-sanctioned marriage may emerge as the single, accepted script. We should anticipate that legal marriage will compel changes in what forms are considered legitimate ways of recognizing lesbian and gay couples' commitments, reducing the variety of ways partnership is recognized.

In these three ways, I find evidence for the cultural power of marriage to change the everyday lives of gay and lesbian couples and to establish a normative trajectory for their commitments. Although these couples are outside of the heteronormative ideal by virtue of their partner choice, in marriage they are subject to existing patterns of social behavior. Lesbian and gay couples do not change these patterns through their participation in marriage. These experiences of normativity among same-sex couples married in San Francisco—even though their marriages' legality was short lived—underscore the tenacity of the relationship between marriage and heteronormativity.

It Changed My Relationship

To a person, the individuals I spoke with described themselves as fully committed before their San Francisco weddings. Yet despite their previous felt commitment, several respondents remarked incredulously that marriage had changed their relationship. For some, it made them feel their commitment more deeply; for others, it made the relationship feel more stable, creating what Andrew Cherlin (2004) has called enforceable trust; and for still others, it allowed them and their relationship to open up and grow. They did not articulate these as reasons for entering marriage in the first place, nor did they reference a specific person or institution that compelled their relationships to change. Instead, they explained these changes as the result of a sort of invisible force. The city hall weddings provided a unique opportunity for participants not only to hypothesize about how marriage would affect them, but to experience the subtle, embedded social expectations of marriage.

Often, these changes were confusing. For instance, Lynn, the senior center director, was perplexed at the new challenges marriage posed to her then eleven-year relationship. The psychological impact of her marriage to Anne, the artist, was so great that it was as if they were just starting their relationship. Lynn said, "They say the first year of marriage is very challenging and with everything—we'd been together for eleven years—and I totally felt it. I remember calling up my friend and I said to her, 'Everything's different. I don't know what's going on.' She said, 'You just got married.' And I was like, 'Really?' She's like, 'Yes.'" When asked what was different about being married, compared to their previous commitment, Lynn explained, "It's like everything got more serious. With marriage, I just felt more commitment and I felt more permanence." Like every other interviewee, Lynn and her spouse lived together prior to the weddings—Lynn and Anne actually owned their home together—and had made plans for spending their future together, but marriage nonetheless represented something new that Lynn never expected. She described their post-marriage commitment as more advanced than their prior commitment, in ways she never could have conceived. She said, "It just feels like there's another level or something that I didn't know was even there. I thought I was totally committed, but it was like I felt it even deeper when we got married.

It made me feel it even more in a whole new way." Getting married helped Lynn to see Anne as, simply, her family.

Especially in a context where their biological families have not always supported them, this was a break-through for Lynn. In this unanticipated role as Anne's family, Lynn found herself newly cognizant of their interdependence. She considered their money and health to be shared resources now, whereas before she had not thought about either too much. Unlike before their marriage, despite their long-standing joint checking account, Lynn said "Now we really talk to each other more about financial decisions that we're making." And when Lynn was contemplating medical treatment for her spine, it was important to her that Anne participate in that decision-making, although previously she might have moved forward on her own while still apprising Anne of her plan.

For Lynn, the cultural expectations of marriage made her individual experience of their relationship into something entirely new. Tim and Keith, together seventeen years, did not experience their marriage as dramatically reorienting their relationship, but they did emphasize the way it deepened their commitment to one another. Both men saw marriage as something that transformed their commitment. Keith, the lawyer, described the formal and public process of marriage as impacting their commitment, saying, "I think it actually helped us cement commitment in a way. Even though you've been together a long time, there's something very powerful about having said the vows to each other, looking at each other with witnesses—I guess they weren't family and friends. I think that it's [commitment is] something that it [the marriage] helps. The support helps strengthen the commitment." Tim, despite feeling "already married," also felt the process was significant—and he was surprised at how significant. He said, "There was kind of a surprise for us as a couple—here I'm saying again—who'd been together for seventeen years but had never had a ceremony of any sort, had nonetheless been living together as an extremely committed—if you will, we were living together as married—but had never had a ceremony, had never exchanged formal vows or not in a really clear way articulated that commitment to each other. And there we were.... It was very profound. It was very moving. And it was unexpected."

Just as Keith referenced the importance of witnessing, other couples also spoke in ways that suggest that the cultural mandate of marriage had consequences for their relationships. Sophie, the graduate
student, said of her marriage to Lal, after six years together, "We were
seen committing by other people. They knew we were married now,
too. It was like we were being held—and I think that is part of the
social contract, that you are being held. Other people are witnessing
you saying you're going to be together." The presence of others in their
commitments pushed these couples to further commit to one another,
illustrating the way in which the culture of a practice shapes our psychological expectations and reactions. From their immersion in a
heteronormative society, respondents *knew* that marriage was about
commitment, and enacting a wedding encouraged many to take their
commitment more seriously.

Research on the difference between cohabitation and marriage
among different-sex couples suggests that this experience of marriage as
a gateway is not unique to the couples married in San Francisco. Study-
ing the emergence of adulthood, Jeffery Arnett (2004) finds that adults
experience cohabitation—even extended, committed cohabitation—as
different from marriage. He interprets this outcome as the direct result
of the public nature of marriage. This public component compels a
psychological change in its participants that makes them "feel different" about the relationship. Ultimately, Arnett contends that spouses
gain a sense of security in marriage that changes the dynamics of the
relationship. The stories of Lynn, Keith, Tim, and Sophie suggest this
can be true for same-sex couples, too.

For other respondents, marriage and its cultural expectations
brought individual feelings of relief to their relationships by offering
a script of legitimacy. Frank and Henry had been together for fifty
years at the time of their city hall ceremony. Their relationship sur-
vived distance, homophobic challenges, and years of closeting. And
yet, until their marriage, Frank acknowledges, their relationship was
partly in shadows. This caused some tension between them. Their
city hall wedding opened something up, according to Frank. He said,
"It made us proud, made us more open about our relationship. Just
between us, it changed things. We didn't fight as much. We were more
caring. We were more loving. What I saw from my partner's point

of view, from my point of view towards my partner, he just became really sweet, much sweeter than he'd ever been in his entire life." Frank sounded this theme throughout his interview, finally summing up, "I'll give you another sentence here: It changed the dynamics of our relationship." With the cultural legitimacy of marriage, Henry could be proud of his commitment to Frank. Frank explained, "My partner was always rather embarrassed when somebody would ask how long we'd been together. He didn't like talking about how long we'd been together. From then on he started saying, 'Fifty years!'" Legal marriage gave Frank and Henry the cultural endorsement that allowed Henry, in particular, to overcome his own psychological barriers—and perhaps internalized homophobia—about their relationship.

Once formally married, respondents experienced many of the modern emotional "benefits" of marriage. Janet, for example, explained that the city hall wedding had strengthened her security in her relationship, providing her with what Cherlin (2004) terms enforceable trust. Now that Janet and Cynthia were married, after twelve years together, Janet felt differently about their relationship. Like Lynn, she referenced an additional level of commitment available through marriage, saying, "I guess in some sense [marriage] made us more committed. [It] moved our relationship to a next level. Not that we weren't committed before, but it was moved to another level. The commitment was more." Of course, even as Janet embraced the emotional comfort marriage afforded her, Cynthia pointed out that she did not have the same experience. She told me that marriage did not change her experience of her relationship to Janet. Still, she acknowledged that the formal process of marriage made Janet feel more secure.

Addy and Julie, together three years before their marriage, told a similar story of give and take following their city hall wedding. Julie felt that she relinquished some of her independence after they married, but she was not quite sure why. She said, "I didn't *have* to relinquish independence. It wasn't like, OK, now I can't be as independent anymore. But I think, for some reason, I did. It wasn't like, 'Oh, you can't be independent anymore,' or that we had a conversation where we said that. I think I just did. I think I became more open." Meanwhile, Addy explained that she agreed that Julie had become more open after their wedding, but, unexpectedly, Julie's openness mattered less to Addy once they married. Julie relinquished some independence, Addy said, "But [also she] didn't because I realized that she could be more independent and I don't have to worry about her leaving me." For Addy, marriage meant she did not need the same level of mutual dependence to feel secure in her relationship, while Julie experienced marriage as something that compelled increased openness.

None of these respondents could pinpoint the source of these newfound dynamics more precisely than to cite their participation in marriage. These couples had many years—sometimes even decades—of commitment under their belts, and yet marriage changed their relationships.

Not all respondents embraced the changes marriage brought on with open arms. Sonia, the public employee, expressed regret for the commitment enforcement that accompanied marriage. At the time of our interview, she and her wife were in the process of going their separate ways, but their marriage (despite it being legally void at the time of the interview) made the relationship substantially more difficult to dissolve. Sonia explained, "I think getting married did create problems because even after we received the paperwork that the marriage was null and void [in August 2004], it still wasn't to us. And so then we went and did the domestic partnership. I don't think that either of us researched the whole thing to really understand the implications. We are now getting a divorce." Sonia believed that many of the complications of dissolving her relationship stemmed from their decision to get married. She said, "In a lot of ways, [having married] made us continue in a situation that we knew was not in our best interest because we didn't want to be a statistic, because we didn't want to have a failed marriage." Sonia explained that their concern was not for the precarious position of gay marriage and their status as a lesbian couple. It was, she said, "just about the marriage." Marriage carried expectations of working out differences and Sonia took those expectations seriously.

Participation in marriage compelled several of my respondents to engage in the cultural tool kit (Swidler 1986) of what it means to be married. In reporting changes in their relationships, despite years of previous commitment, interviewees signaled the cultural impact of normative narratives of marriage and its meaning on personal behavior and perception. Marriage is not something these couples just entered; their participation in the city hall weddings also meant that at least some of the expectations of marriage entered them. For many, these expectations were a positive thing; for others like Sonia, the relationship reorientation that came with marriage was a negative thing.

Living Married

Outside of the couple, marriage changed the way respondents moved through the world. They reported that marriage changed the way the law treated them, shifted some of their interactions with corporate entities, and served to orient social behavior toward them in inclusive ways. While only some interviewees articulated ways marriage had changed their relationship to their partner, every person I spoke with identified at least one way his or her status as married changed their interaction with others. In their day-to-day experience, the ways marriage mattered were extensive, spanning workplace interactions, family relationships, and friendships.

To start, marriage changed the way they interacted with the state and other institutions. Respondents had immediate access to some of the standard benefits of legal marriage, like ease of surname change. Phoebe, the analyst from Southern California, for instance, used her marriage certificate to expedite a name change on her social security card to her wife's surname.

> We came back that Saturday, and that Monday morning I was at the social security office with my marriage license. I handed my marriage license to the lady behind the counter and she sort of looked at me and looked down at the paper and then looked at me again. And then she said, "This is one of those, isn't it?" And I said, "It's a marriage license." And then she said, "But you married a female, right?" And I said, "Yes, I married a female." And then she goes, "I have to talk to my supervisor." And she ran off around the corner and talked with her supervisor and then came back and gave me my receipt, saying my name was changed. It was relatively painless.

Of course, some benefits of marriage remained unavailable. Because the 1996 DOMA prevents the federal government from recognizing

same-sex marriages, Tim and Keith were still unable to file joint federal tax returns as they so ardently wished.

Marriage also enabled participants to gain access to quasi-legal
privileges, such as spousal health-care coverage, that are reserved for
married couples and doled out by non-state institutions (for example,
employers). For example, Elizabeth, the accounting assistant, had long
wanted to include Laura on her workplace-issued health insurance,
but company policy extended coverage only to married spouses, not
domestic partners. Upon returning to work just hours after their wedding, Elizabeth's first action was to request health insurance coverage
for Laura: "After we went down to the city and got married, I called up
the HR department and said, 'I need to come see you.' And I went in
there and told them, 'Well, we're married. I want to fill out the forms
for coverage.'" Similarly, some respondents sought other marriage-
related workplace perks, such as discount cards. Chris, the marketing
manager, said, "It's kind of dumb—I work for a retail company and
I immediately said, 'Alan can now get a discount.'" With a marriage
certificate—and the state support it entailed—participants in the San
Francisco weddings were able to access workplace benefits that were
otherwise unavailable to them.

Scholars of (different-sex) marriage and family have documented
other workplace-based benefits of marriage, such as a marital wage
benefit. White, married men, for example, have been shown to experience a wage benefit associated with marital status (Cohen 2002;
Korenman and Neumark 1991). These benefits, however, are not experienced across race categories (Glauber 2008; Loh 1996). Scholars
have similarly shown evidence of a wage penalty for women based
on their marital status (Avellar and Smock 2003; Budig and England
2001; Glauber 2007; Waldfogel 1997). This research on the wage benefit
experienced by white, married men both offers evidence of additional
monetary consequences of marital status and poses an open question
as to whether same-sex marriage will translate in the same way into a
wage benefit.

Susan's story of her separation from her partner, Dawn, a year or so
after their 2004 San Francisco wedding illustrates the importance of
legal marriage in a different way. Susan, the librarian, and Dawn broke
up after their wedding license had been ruled invalid. But, according to

Susan, she played little part in the process. In Susan's retelling, Dawn had a mental breakdown but kept her deterioration from Susan. Dawn confided in her therapist and psychiatrist, both of whom judged that she should be in the hospital, but Dawn persuaded them to allow her to stay out of the hospital as long as she was with a designated monitor twenty-four hours a day. Both health professionals allowed Dawn to designate a woman she had met only a few months earlier—not Susan—as this monitor. Susan was never consulted or apprised of Dawn's situation. Respectful of Dawn's privacy, Susan recognized that the therapist and psychiatrist could not have required that Susan be Dawn's monitor, but she was incensed that they permitted this other woman to perform that role. She said, "That wouldn't have happened if we were a straight, married couple. They would either have insisted it be me or that she be in the hospital." Two years after the break-up, at the time of our interview, Susan was still confused about what had gone wrong but believed her lack of legal relationship to Dawn contributed to the difficulty of their break-up. She believed that if they had still been married when Dawn left, the process would have been more transparent and offered her more answers. Although advocates rarely cite the protections of the divorce process as a rallying cry for same-sex marriage, Susan's story highlights how some benefits of marriage apply when the relationship is not going well.

Outside of its effect on the state and institutions, legal marriage functioned in everyday interactions as a kind of social currency. Respondents noted positively, for example, the outpouring of support they experienced from coworkers following the wedding events. Ernesto's boss was so supportive that she insisted Ernesto take the day off from work after his morning wedding. Ernesto related, "I was there [at work] in the afternoon. And the word spread that we got married. They were all aware, and the first thing my boss said was, 'What are you doing here?' So she decided I should go home. I should take a day off. I shouldn't work that day. But before that, you know, there was a lot of congratulations. And we took a group picture together. We're all hugging." Many received flowers, cards, and other gifts from coworkers. Sonia, the public employee, described an experience in her workplace that was typical of other respondents' experiences: "Coworkers were very happy, very pleased, very accepting, even some of our

clients—and we work with developmentally disabled. I'm thinking
of one woman in particular. To see her, she appears like somebody
from *Happy Days*, bobby socks, hip-flared skirts, and the whole nine
yards—real straitlaced. And she sent me a card saying: Congratulations and she didn't know why it's anybody's damn business who I
married. It was just a very welcoming kind of situation." Respondents
were rewarded with spoken congratulations, gifts, and days off from
work following their weddings, demonstrating social support for
their act of legally formalizing their relationships. Even when they did
not ask for such treatment, interviewees like Ernesto were persuaded
to treat the days and activities around their marriages reverentially,
abstaining from their everyday responsibilities.

People whom respondents interacted with on a regular basis
tapped into normative scripts about how one reacts to news of
someone's nuptials, instinctively offering congratulations. Anne and
Lynn, of the half-finished coffee on the kitchen table, both remarked
that sometimes this social norm trumped people's personal feelings
about same-sex marriage. Lynn described announcing her marriage
to coworkers whom she anticipated were opposed to same-sex marriage: "It was really important to me to just be myself and to just go
into work and work with some people that are Republicans or whatever and say, 'I just got married today.' And for them to say, 'Oh, congratulations,' and not even blink an eye, because that's what you say
when somebody says, 'I got married today,' whether or not you agree
with them." Anne elaborated on this idea, explaining how the standard discourse of support defines appropriate reactions to marriage
announcements. She said, "When you say you got married, they know
what to do. People know what to do when you say you just got married: 'Congratulations!' No matter who you tell, it doesn't matter. You
say you got married, they understand the concept. It's not something
you have to explain to anybody." Social norms around marriage dictated that others react positively to respondents' wedding news.

Tim and Keith received a great deal of social support for their marriage, even some entirely unexpected support. As Tim, the policy analyst, told the story,

> We did receive a spontaneous outpouring of congratulations and
> gifts and cards. After that had run its course we came home one day,

several weeks later, and there were some flowers on our doorstep and I said, "Oh I wonder who just heard or what this is about." I looked at the card and it was from my best friend from first grade, who had just gotten the news. Her sister was still friends with my sister. Somehow it had worked its way around the country and gotten to her. Just a very simple note with the flowers and it said, "I'm so happy that my best friend from first grade is finally able to get married. Congratulations."

Although Tim had not been in contact with this woman for decades, marriage represented an occasion for contact and celebration. She reached out to him *because* of the marriage and expressed positive sentiments about his relationship to Keith. Without marriage, Tim likely would not have heard from her, let alone received flowers.

The language of marriage prompted particular social responses beyond gifts and exclamations of "congratulations." The state sanction of these relationships socially cued the responses of others in ways that long-term personal commitments had not. Anne has two brothers, neither of whom ever made much effort to get to know Lynn. Anne found herself repeatedly frustrated at the familial expectations that she show up for their weddings, send gifts when new babies arrived, and reward their normative lifestyle when neither brother acknowledged any of her and Lynn's eleven anniversaries. Following their San Francisco wedding, Anne demanded that her brothers send their congratulations and they did. Anne noted that being married "is a time in your life where you feel like you're acknowledged."

Aaron, the attorney, offered a similar explanation for his appreciation of legal marriage. He explained that legal marriage gave him access to a social language of family that is generally understood. He said, "So what it meant to me was really that ability to communicate . . . to be included in the social discourse, to be included in the social lexicon, to be able to identify, using the language of our society, the way I would if I were not excluded from this institution." When Aaron referred to Gabe as his husband, it was shorthand that conveyed their relationship in familiar language. Being married, he said, "helps in terms of social significance." Aaron's explanation shows how the language of marriage has lasting impacts in social discourse, beyond immediate reactions to a wedding announcement, that mark these couples as families.

For a notable few, the legal wedding did more than simply orient the actions of others, it transformed personal relationships. Keith, the lawyer, experienced an exchange with his husband's brother during which the brother seemed to finally recognize Keith and Tim's relationship. He related, "I think that one thing that was so striking about the wedding was how this meant something very different to people. They understood it in a way they hadn't before. One example: it wasn't that weekend, but the first time I think we saw [Tim's brother] physically after the wedding—we had just shown him some of [our photos from the wedding]—and he said, 'Oh my God. My God. I have a brother-in-law.' I've known this person for decades. It was just that now he conceptualized it differently."

For Janet and Cynthia, although their families knew of their twelve-year relationship and the two had held a commitment ceremony, it was not until after their legal wedding that Janet felt fully embraced by Cynthia's family. Janet explained, "They all knew [about our relationship] and they were all fine with it. But when we actually announced it [our marriage], her family was all thrilled. 'Oh, let's throw a party.' 'Oh, here, send cards.' 'Oh here, we gotta do something!' We married in February and, in May, we went to her niece's wedding in Florida and they were all celebrating and congratulating us and it was like, 'Okay. This is good.'" Marriage gave respondents' families a language and cultural context in which to interpret these committed same-sex relationships. Sometimes, it facilitated closer bonds, showing how marriage cues others to particular understandings of same-sex relationships. Legal marriage changed the way extended family members viewed their relationships, causing participants like Keith and Janet to experience newfound legitimacy in the eyes of people they had known well for years.

Marriage mattered in some respondents' interpersonal family relationships as well. Although they had been together for six years before their 2004 wedding and co-raised both Isabel's and Raine's biological daughters, Isabel had always felt some distance between herself and Raine's daughter. That changed after the San Francisco wedding:

> It changed my relationship with my partner's daughter. I don't
> know what happened, but it affected both of us. It became a more
> legitimate I'm your step-mom, you're my step-kid sort of thing after

marriage. . . . I don't even know how to explain it or what happened. It's just like something opened in both of us that wasn't able to open before. And that is my favorite thing from the whole experience was that that was able to happen. . . . I still don't understand that. And it doesn't matter that I don't [laughs]. It's just a beautiful thing. I don't think that would've happened without the actual marriage.

Marriage served to reorient Isabel and her stepdaughter's relationship, enabling them to draw closer together and feel more solidly like family. The cultural symbolism of marriage extended beyond the experiences of the couples to encompass their entire family units, often in entirely unexpected but profound ways. For respondents like Isabel who experienced this ripple, while they perhaps could not explain the effect, they were nonetheless highly aware of the social impacts of state-sanctioned marriage.

Marriage was an orienting touchstone for Michelle and Kelly's son, Andrew, as well. Andrew was not quite two years old when his mothers married, and they brought him with them to city hall. Standing in line was stressful, as they tried to keep him entertained and worried about how he would hold up without his regular nap, but the chance to marry seemed worth it. Andrew was too young to remember their wedding, but they talk about it with him often, telling him he was their best man. Age five when I interviewed Michelle and Kelly, Andrew retells the wedding story regularly, sometimes prompted by seeing a building that looks even just a little bit like San Francisco's city hall. As Kelly explained, "We tell him he'll always be our best man. That's part of our family story now." In these stories of changing family relationships we find most clearly evidence of the power of the institution of marriage to make manifest certain relationships and, in so doing, orient the actions of others.

In terms of personal relationships, workplace policies, and everyday social interactions, as the interview data illustrate, legal marriage changes the relationships and relative positions of gay and lesbian individuals. The experience of the weddings carried beyond the city hall ceremonies into the lives of the participants and did so in overwhelmingly positive ways. Most simply, with marriage the couples accrued legal rights. More complexly, the institutional sanction of the state served to orient the behavior of others, whether strangers,

in-laws, or their children, to recognize committed same-sex relationships (although other work on same-sex marriage demonstrates the
possibility of negative social consequences; see Ocobock 2013).

Often unintentionally, marriage was a way for participants to
display themselves as families, and numerous respondents reported
that this public experience of display led others to recognize them
as families. The San Francisco weddings offered what Janet Finch
(2007) describes as a narrative to communicate family relationships
to multiple audiences, from the law to members of their communities, including friends, coworkers, and even those they already called
family. In marrying, these relationships moved into the public realm,
where they were no longer simply done, but *seen to be done*. For many
respondents, marriage was initially simply a status. But its repeated
emergence outside of city hall in the fields of the law, the workplace,
and the family suggests that it saturated participants' lives, becoming
not just a status but an orienting identity.

These experiences underscore the social difference between marriage and civil unions, offering insight into why the same package
of benefits under a different name (civil unions) is not equivalent to
marriage. Whereas social discourses accompany marriage, no such
norms exist around civil unions. There are no conventions about how
others are supposed to react to a civil union. It is marriage itself, not
the package of legal rights it encompasses, that is symbolically potent.

Decreasing Commitment Practices

Thus far in this chapter, I have shown ways legal marriage grants same-
sex couples access to previously unavailable scripts. Next, I turn to the
possibility that legal marriage can also make other kinds of existing
scripts obsolete, or at least illegitimate, by looking at respondents'
pre–San Francisco marriage commitment ceremonies. Without the
ability to secure legal sanction, lesbian and gay couples have created a
number of ways to celebrate their commitments. Indeed, the majority
of my interviewees (N = 32; 76 percent) held commitment ceremonies
prior to their San Francisco weddings. While many of the components
of these ceremonies, and in some cases the entire ceremony save for
the legal recognition, map onto legal weddings, not all do. Some have

more in common with normative definitions of an engagement rather than a wedding, and others lack even the minimal formal planning an elopement would require. Still other respondents abstained entirely from a ceremony.

Legal marriage, I suggest, will delegitimize these scripts, compelling lesbian and gay couples to conform to normative commitment practices. M. V. Lee Badgett (2009) has termed this a shift from a do-it-yourself model to "off-the-rack" commitment. As Barry Adam (2004, 273) notes, same-sex marriage is about assimilating same-sex relationships into existing law and cultural practice, rather than integrating these families as they are into recognized statuses. For couples whose ceremonies share much in common with legal marriage ceremonies, this assimilation is incremental. However, other scripts may no longer be legitimate when marriage is available. And the absence of a formal commitment all together may become suspect or be considered a stepping-stone phase, as many different-sex, cohabiting couples already experience.

No Commitment Ceremony

Among the interviewees there was a range of relationship solemnization rituals, as well as the election—sometimes active, sometimes passive—*not* to engage in any sort of formal ceremony recognizing their commitment to one another. These couples did not create a benchmark for their commitment, entering into shared home ownership, merged finances, and numerous other trappings of long-term commitment without notable occasion. They chose this path for a variety of reasons. For some, it was a conscious decision. Terrance, now retired, did not like the restrictions any marriage-like ceremony had on relationships and had rejected the idea of a commitment ceremony both in his current long-term relationship and in his prior seventeen-year-long relationship. While both of his long-term relationships have been monogamous, he objected to the idea that "someone else" would make rules about his romantic life. He thought of commitment ceremonies as forcing relationships to conform to a standard couple structure, something he perceived as "someone else putting their own thoughts on your relationship. The reality is it's not for them to do. It's for you to do." Indeed, he called commitment ceremonies the "kiss of death" for gay relationships and noted that nearly every gay or lesbian couple he knew who had a commitment ceremony separated a few years later.

Keith and Tim, already married in their eyes, with seventeen years of commitment, similarly actively decided not to have a commitment ceremony, but their decision owed to the non-legal status of such ceremonies. Keith explained, "We thought about it some. Through complicated events with family, it wasn't clear we would be able to have exactly what we wanted. But then it became more that we don't want to do this. We don't want something that's half-baked. We want something that's real and fully legal. We're not going to do it until that's the case."

Others intended to have a ceremony but things never quite fell into place. Frank and Henry, together fifty years, tried to have a commitment ceremony several times, never successfully. In one instance, they joined up with four other gay couples (one pair of gay men and three lesbian couples), but, as Frank explained, "It fell apart mainly because everybody wanted something different. Everybody had different ideas of what a commitment ceremony should be: should it be like marriage? Should it be something else? Should you say your own personal vows? It sort of just died away, much to my disappointment." Another time they attempted to coordinate a commitment ceremony, it was just going to be the two of them, but that never came to fruition either. Despite their repeated attempts and Frank's interest, Henry was not particularly motivated to have a commitment ceremony. As Frank related, "Henry's response was always 'why?' He says, 'Isn't fifty years together enough of a commitment?'"

For still others, life just got in the way. While actively socialist in her own leanings and avowedly against the institution of marriage, Barbara, the electrician, conceded that her partner, Gayle, had probably always been interested in having a commitment ceremony. Gayle was, as Barbara explained, "Not so keen on marriage but keen on rites and rituals." Barbara explained that there was never a particular moment when the issue came up in their three years together, so they had never made a decision one way or the other on having a ceremony.

Weddings without Legal Sanction

Another set of couples held commitment ceremonies, and their ceremonies took several forms, all of which have analogies to commitment recognitions by heterosexual couples. Small or large, these ceremonies conformed to at least some traditional wedding conventions. Sandra and Olivia held their commitment ceremony in their local community center and invited friends and family. Olivia, the programmer, said, "Her sister stood up for her. My stepfather stood up for me. My father is in Spain, so he doesn't get to participate in these things really. All of her family was there. My grandfather and his second wife were there. My mom's twin brother and his daughter were there." Deidre and Leslie were married in their backyard. Chris and Alan married at Alan's parents' home in Northern California in what was, according to Alan, "a very large, basically wedding [laughs] at my parents' house."

For some respondents, the ceremony was expressly intended to parallel a traditional wedding. Philip said of his ceremony with Steven that, minus the dresses, "We wanted to try to make it as 'traditional wedding' as possible. Sometimes when we've heard of ceremonies, it's more of—we'll go to city hall and do something with a couple people. But we always like to party, so we wanted to make it as traditional as possible, with the flowers, with the cake, with the dinner, with our friends, with our family, with the music, just pretty much [the] same as any other wedding." In some cases, the traditional format took religious form. Susan had what she described as "a pretty traditional Jewish wedding," and Craig described his ceremony as "a big old church wedding" with over four hundred attendees.

Although these ceremonies borrowed from heterosexual wedding conventions, the adaptation was not without some wrinkles. For some of these couples, their commitment ceremony *felt* different from what they imagined a wedding would feel like. Couples felt that, by definition, same-sex ceremonies were not real weddings. For instance, Alan remembers discussing what he and Chris would call their commitment event: "We used 'commitment ceremony' for a long time, which is funny. That kind of stems from the knowledge that we can't get married, I think, in one way. Calling it a wedding is naming it something it isn't, yet it is." Chris elaborated, "At that point, most of our friends were straight and obviously accepting of us. But because we were in this unknown territory, I didn't want to get a confrontation with someone of like, 'Why are you calling it a wedding? It's not a real wedding.' Or whatever. So it was really almost part nervousness

on our part also." Alan and Chris had the desire to have an elaborate
ceremony that was like a wedding but felt that it simply could not *be* a
wedding because there were two grooms.

Even as these ceremonies adopted conventions from traditional
weddings, many were, in their own ways, nontraditional. At Craig and
Stanley's "big old church wedding," they were married by their Unitar-
ian minister and a Buddhist priest in a joint ceremony, adapting the
traditional form of a church wedding to meet their personal requirements. Isabel and Raine, who met in the Mormon Church, looked
outside the church but not outside of spiritual symbolism to formalize their commitment. They chose to conduct a Native American ceremony called a blessing way, held in what Isabel described as a "little
white southern church in Georgia":

> What your friends do is they take a colored ribbon—they're all col-
> ors of the rainbow since the rainbow tribe is, you know, the Native
> American tribe—and they take a colored ribbon and they take a
> piece of paper and they write what they want you to be blessed
> with or what their wishes are for you. And they roll it up and tie it
> with the ribbon. And then all of these ribbons get tied on this stick
> and that becomes part of the ceremony—we both hold it during
> the ceremony. And then every anniversary, you can take that down
> and read all the little blessings and it reminds you of what you were
> wished when you got married. So it's a neat little, continues-to-
> keep-giving kind of experience.

Isabel felt that the format of their ceremony suited them as individuals
and as a couple, even if it drew from non-mainstream elements.

Couples spoke of the events as touchstones for their relationships,
a memory to return to that infused their relationship with greater
importance and meaning. Key to the invested importance of these
ceremonies was their public nature, the fact that the couple said
their vows in front of an audience. As Steven explained of his and
Philip's "traditional" ceremony, "We were pretty happy even before
that, but it really steps up the level of commitment that you have
made to say that everybody was there, everybody was part of that
whole thing. If we let [our relationship] disintegrate, that's really a
crime. It's really, if we allowed something to come between us now,

it would have to be really a serious thing. We've said that we're going to work it out. We've said that we're going to make it a priority. . . . There's just a different flavor to the commitment once you had all of your friends and family witness that kind of thing. I think it brought us closer together." For Philip and Steven, the power of marriage was conferred on their relationship through their commitment ceremony, even without the legal document, by the witnessing of their friends and family. In some ways, they insisted on their commitment regardless of legality. Steven related, "At one point in our wedding ceremony, our officiant said something to the effect of that we're not waiting for someone else or some government or some court somewhere to say what we're going to do with our lives and we want to have this because we want it to be shared with each other and with all of our family and friends."

Deidre, the writer, also emphasized the public nature of her commitment to Leslie, citing it as central to the reason that they opted to have a ceremony and of vital importance to the health and longevity of their commitment itself: "I guess [our reasons for having a commitment ceremony are] threefold: wanting to voice our commitment to each other; wanting to celebrate that we found each other; and then also wanting to ask our community for support because, you know, marriage isn't the easiest thing and sometimes you need your friends to kick you in the butt a couple times to remind you what you're there for and all that good stuff." The experience of witnesses was integral to the value these respondents ascribed to formalizing their commitment. Although many of these formal ceremonies were nontraditional, we can easily see their similarity to legal marriage ceremonies. These were weddings without a marriage license.

Speaking Commitment to Each Other

Others opted for ceremonies without the presence of others, formalizing their commitment to one another in an explicitly personal, private way. Several interview respondents participated in commitment ceremonies that involved only the couple. These ceremonies held as much meaning and importance to the relationship as those described above but did not include family and friends or even an official to bless or solemnize their commitment. Instead, couples shared their commitments only with one another, creating ceremonies that had unique and express importance to them alone.

In some cases, these private ceremonies were carefully planned. After a year together, Dale and Pierre decided to formalize their commitment to one another. They spent two months picking out rings, checked into a four-star hotel a few miles from their home, ordered room service, and relaxed in their bathrobes, committing to each other according to their own script. Dale, the nightclub manager, explained, "We just basically sat down and expressed our love to each other and exchanged little cheap-y ten dollar rings—we had the [real] rings with us that we had bought already, but they weren't properly sized, so I bought some cheap little silver bands, something to wear in the meantime and something to go ahead and do our exchange at that point in time." On their own terms, they created a ceremony that was meaningful to them and their relationship.

Anne and Lynn traveled farther from home, to Hawaii, to hold their very amorphous, private commitment ceremony. They each had rings, but only loose plans of what their ceremony would entail. In the end, the entire trip became their ceremony. Lynn, the senior center director, explained, "It just kind of evolved. It wasn't a date kind of thing. We went [to Hawaii] and we weren't exactly sure what we were going to do, but we knew we were going to do something. It just kind of evolved. It wasn't like we planned exactly how it was going to work. We would be at some incredible place and then we would just say things to each other about our commitment to each other." Anne elaborated, "We built a cairn, which is a pile of rocks, with a flower on top in the [shadow] of the volcano and left that there as kind of a monument to us—that we were there and having a commitment. We took a picture of it. We just did stuff like that that was more kind of an extended ceremony." With some financial motivation—Anne said, "it's not like we could afford to fly all our friends to Hawaii to be with us"—a great deal of creativity, and no standard restrictive model, as Anne said, "We just did it on our own."

In other cases, the commitment ceremony was a planned surprise by one member of the couple. Brian's partner, Robert, surprised him with rings on a weekend getaway, and Brian, the lawyer, explained, "We had our own sort of private ceremony and got married." The two consider that day their anniversary. Janet, the nurse, similarly surprised Cynthia in what she called "another not-quite-planned, sort-of-planned idea." Janet led Cynthia on an uncharacteristic hike—"Normally, I don't go across the parking lot"—in Glacier Park, where the two were participating in a square-dancing retreat. At the top, she presented Cynthia with a set of silver earrings in what they consider their commitment ceremony. Janet explained, "We went off to the side, did a little talking to each other, exchanged the earrings, and then had to climb down because it's going to be dark!" Although nontraditional, this event became symbolic to both Janet and Cynthia of their commitment to each other.

Finally, in contrast to ceremonies planned by one or both members of the couple, for some couples, their commitment ceremony was entirely impromptu. Following their registration as domestic partners, Sophie and Lal had what Sophie, the graduate student, described as "an impromptu ceremony." She explained, "We had had a very small, just the two of us ceremony when she asked me to marry her. We went to dinner with our friends after and then we actually went away for a little honeymoon the next day, up to wine country." With no prior discussion or planning, the two comfortably embarked on what they both considered their marriage ceremony. Addy and Julie's unplanned but relationship-orienting commitment took place without them even leaving their home. Addy explained, "Julie and I were in bed one night. We were close to each other and she told me that she promises to take care of me no matter what, that my heart is safe with her, and then I promised her the same thing. That was our commitment ceremony. Then we gave each other the same rings that we've been wearing for a long time. Took them off each other's finger and handed them back, put them on our fingers." For Addy and Julie, although they had been wearing rings symbolic of their commitment "for a long time," their spoken commitment in bed was their commitment touchstone.

Although their commitments weren't witnessed by friends or family, these couples insisted that they were just as significant as a public event. When asked how his private commitment ceremony differed from a more public recognition, Pierre, the Canadian citizen, said, "I think it was different because it wasn't public, but the meaning was the same." Others emphasized that their private ceremonies were centrally about them and their relationship. Lynn, for instance, said, "Well, for me, getting married on the big island of Hawaii was really just about us. It wasn't about anybody else." Indeed, for Addy, it was the impromptu, private nature of the event that made it so meaningful. She said, "I think that [the spontaneity of our commitment is] something that makes me value that ceremony more than anything else. That one came out of the heart and came from nowhere. It was something we were feeling at the moment." Without access to traditional marriage, these couples devised their own, personally meaningful ceremonies.

For at least one couple, Michelle and Kelly, the choice to hold an entirely private ceremony was made explicitly in the political context in which same-sex marriage was unavailable. While Keith and Tim opted out of any kind of ceremony until legal marriage was an option, Kelly, the professor, and Michelle, the accountant, decided to formally celebrate their commitment when they were ready to become parents—but since it could not be legal, they did not include anyone else. Kelly explained: "We decided to just have a private ceremony because it wasn't legal. And we wanted it eventually legal."

Michelle and Kelly drove north from San Francisco to Mendocino County for a semi-scripted commitment ceremony on their one-year anniversary, on a beach in the wee hours of the morning to assure their privacy. They had a script for the event that borrowed from more conventional ceremonies but nonetheless remained entirely private. Their ceremony included meaningful objects such as a quilt from Michelle's parents and thirteen candles to celebrate a number of significance to their relationship. For their ceremony, Kelly explained, "We had both written vows that we kept secret from each other until then. We had already ordered rings that we had inscribed on the inside—we kept the messages secret for each other, too. We exchanged vows just on the beach by ourselves in the morning." In this way, the witnessing of their commitment was by them alone and not friends and family, even though both described themselves as close to their families.

As Michelle and Kelly constructed their commitment ceremony in opposition to a social field wherein same-sex marriage was unavailable, so too were the other couples who engaged in private commitment ceremonies writing their own scripts in the absence of a culturally formalized one. Under more traditional terms, none of these ceremonies would be recognized as marriages and several, like Addy and Julie's nighttime commitment while lying in bed, would barely register as engagements. Mapping the language of different-sex marriage onto these stories, some of the commitment ceremonies would be understood as engagements, especially those in which one member surprised the other. Still others might be understood as honeymoons, such as Anne and Lynn's adventure in Hawaii. Yet these couples experienced these practices as their commitment ceremonies, both at the time and for many years afterward. Some spurned friends and family, actively keeping the event private, while others voiced their commitment only by happenstance. Some planned far ahead, some exchanged rings, some wrote vows, and all experienced that event as a touchstone in their relationship that marked their commitment to one another. In essence, these couples rewrote the rules on commitment, creating their own scripts.

When Legal Marriage Is Available

The availability of marriage to same-sex couples presages a cultural shift in how couples recognize their commitments. Lesbian and gay couples will be expected to formalize their commitments through marriage, and this represents a loss in the diversity of commitment recognition scripts. While some gay and lesbian commitment ceremonies mirror the admittedly varied content of different-sex weddings, many of the ceremonies respondents described do not so easily map onto traditional heterosexual weddings. Instead, several took a unique form that intentionally lacked any third-party official.

When legal same-sex marriage is available, same-sex couples and others are likely to find these nontraditional commitment scripts less legitimate. As lesbian and gay couples no longer write their own rules and instead have community, historical, and state standards to conform to, they will be expected to commit to each other in public, rather than private. Couples who formerly created their own path may increasingly opt for the path of legitimation. Insofar as existing commitment ceremonies mimic conventional weddings and receptions, the ceremonies themselves can be easily adapted—incorporated— into legal weddings. Indeed, some respondents' express goal in their commitment ceremony was to have a (non-legal) wedding. It is unlikely, however, that private ceremonies will be similarly adapted

under state sanctioning. Instead, we can expect the disappearance or
at least decrease of private marriage ceremonies.

It is also not unreasonable to anticipate the decrease in long-term
relationships that exist without any formalized commitment ceremony. Just as some couples will feel social pressure to conform to certain standards of commitment ceremony, we can anticipate that other
couples will feel social pressure to conform to certain standards of
commitment itself, namely, its formalization. Couples will no longer
be able to go seventeen years without really thinking about formalizing their commitment, as Keith and Tim did. Marriage, as Suzanna
Walters (2001) argues, may become compulsory in the gay and lesbian
community. This is a notable shift in how same-sex couples inter-
face with broader society. The partial extinction of alternative scripts
means the lesbian and gay community loses one means of speaking
back to heteronormative expectations of commitment.

THE HEGEMONY OF HETERONORMATIVE MARRIAGE

Although gays and lesbians offered a range of meanings for marriage, often explicitly articulating meanings that contested heteronormativity, the institution of marriage acted on them in ways they
did not always anticipate. Respondents who did not marry in order to
gain security and deeper commitment felt those effects nonetheless.
After marrying, Anne and Lynn felt a firmer sense of commitment
and a sense of family. Janet felt more secure. Henry became more
open about his relationship with Frank. Outside of their marriages,
social norms dictated how institutions, coworkers, family, and friends
engaged with the couples. Respondents were rewarded for marrying,
receiving social encouragement for their participation in the institution. With marriage, these couples were treated as ordinary couples.
They were treated as normative.

In these ways, any challenge to heteronormativity by the practice
of same-sex marriage is seemingly neutralized. Respondents' stories
offer evidence of the triumph of normativity—and the possibility of its
extension. Beyond the predicted loss of alternative commitment scripts,
another possible consequence of legal same-sex marriage is the further
marginalization of certain kinds of relationships. Not only do some

existing ceremonies more easily fit into the tradition of legal marriage, so too do some gay and lesbian relationships more easily assimilate to cultural expectations about who participates in state sanction. Judith Butler (2002) has cautioned that an immediate effect of legal same-sex marriage is that it will render some, but not all, lesbian and gay relationships legitimate. Those relationships close to the margins of legitimacy may be encouraged through social expectation to conform to normative standards such as marriage, but those relationships far from the margins of legitimacy may be rendered even less legitimate. The respectable same-sex couples Mariana Valverde (2006) writes about who focus on issues of child-rearing and finances rather than sexuality may easily gain access to the benefits of the state, and the so-called good gays may receive social encouragement (Walters 2001), but what of those who do not fit into these legitimate categories?

Taking a larger view, the impacts of the perpetuation of normative marriage may extend beyond gay and lesbian couples to reduce the proliferation of commitment scripts and relationship forms for people of all sexual identities. Wendy Langford (1999) points to our social dependence on the couple as an organizing unit, illustrating how it has been constructed as the primary location of meaning and self-worth. As alternative scripts of how coupledom is made are lost, we can also surmise that alternative forms of relationships outside of the monogamous, dyadic couple are simultaneously being lost. The adoption of formal marriage as a practice in the lesbian and gay community may represent a loss of the fluidity of sexual and romantic relationships, or even a loss of "queerness" (Valverde 2006).

Respondents were often surprised by the impacts of marriage on their interpersonal relationships—and often pleased. Even those who intellectually critiqued marriage as a heterosexual practice experienced pleasure in being treated as normative. What this suggests is that the heteronormative character of marriage is only partially recognized. To truly destabilize the relationship between heteronormativity and marriage, the critique must delve deeper into the practice of marriage. Without an intentional critique, the appeal of normativity can paper over the production of privilege. Same-sex couples' practice of marriage may hold the possibility of exposing the institution's heteronormative underpinning—but only when we look for it.

CHAPTER 7

EXPOSING
HETERONORMATIVITY

Part of what makes heteronormativity so insidious is its invisible machinations. We don't even notice it at work, making the unequal status of nonheterosexuals appear to be natural (not to mention its raced and classed effects). Chrys Ingraham (1994) calls this the "heterosexual imaginary." Heterosexuality is so effectively integrated into society as normal that we fail to recognize its construction. In turn, heteronormativity, as a practice that (re)institutes heterosexuality as the norm, is unrecognized. Heteronormativity can be recognized when its invisible machinations are disrupted. Little can be done to reduce sexual identity–based inequality when the processes that institute it remain invisible. Heteronormativity must be moved out of the imaginary and into focus in order to unmake heterosexual privilege.

In key ways, the San Francisco weddings made aspects of heteronormativity visible. More importantly, they exposed the unexpected depths of heteronormativity in everyday life. Respondents' reports of their emotional experiences of marrying in city hall offer one example of how the weddings highlight how same-sex couples' experience is overshadowed by inequality. They spoke of feeling safe, included, and relief from shame, emotions that decidedly diverge from the emotions generally associated with (different-sex) marriage. Even some of those who thought of themselves as completely adjusted to their marginalized social location were surprised at how their emotional response to wedding revealed the extent to which they had internalized their outsider status. These unexpected emotions evidence what I term, borrowing from Richard Sennett and Jonathan Cobb (1972), the hidden injuries of homophobia and point to the ongoing injury of heteronormativity.

In their qualitative analysis of the experience of class, specifically the working class, Sennett and Cobb argue that the hierarchy of class is perpetuated through the socialized reduction of dignity among working people such that they do not challenge the ways in which their freedom is limited. This experience is largely unnoticed—individuals do not constantly feel judged or inadequate—but operates on a hidden level, wounding their dignity "in order to weaken people's ability to fight against the limits class imposes on their freedom" (Sennett and Cobb 1972, 153). Heteronormativity operates in much the same way to limit the expectations of gays and lesbians as it simultaneously encourages them to internalize feelings of marginalization. When these otherwise unrecognized emotions of shame and relief rose to the surface, respondents realized how deeply heterosexual privilege was integrated into their lives.

The emotional pain some respondents experienced when their marriage licenses were invalidated, several months after the Winter of Love, points to a second way in which the marriages revealed the ongoing injury of heteronormativity. Even as respondents admitted that their initial hopes that the licenses would remain valid were tenuous, the experience of having the licenses voided hurt. This forced them to acknowledge their ongoing feelings of marginalization, even in a place as gay-friendly as the Bay Area.

As they recognized this feeling of marginalization, many felt compelled to fight back, aiming to make discrimination visible to others. For some, this meant shifting the focus of their activism to same-sex marriage. For others, it ignited a spirit of protest that had not existed before the weddings. For the same reasons, the Winter of Love and its aftermath inspired my respondents to agitate for marriage equality; they hoped it would inspire others, gay and straight alike, to recognize the extent of sexual identity–based inequality.

At this still early stage of the marriage equality movement, it is hard to measure the effects of this exposure and acknowledgment of heteronormativity. The San Francisco marriages may not have ushered in the dramatic changes some have hoped for, but they do bring the personal effects of heteronormativity into relief and help us trace the dramatic scope of its influence. The institution of marriage acts on the lives of gays and lesbians, perhaps even in ways they want, but their experience of marriage also exposes the previously unnoticed reach of heterosexual privilege.

An Outpouring of Emotion

Weddings are often freighted with emotion, but the emotions respondents experienced during their San Francisco weddings were decidedly different from those anticipated at heterosexual weddings. Many respondents talked about feeling nervous, but they were not nervous about their pending commitment. Instead, participants explained that they were anxious that they would not get their turn to be married. They worried that they would be too late. Phoebe, the analyst, explained, "I actually was worried. I felt like I was a criminal who was sneaking in to try and get my little piece of justice or equality or rights before someone came along and yanked them away. That's completely the way I felt standing in line, waiting. The closer we got to the entrance, it was like, 'OK, we're gonna make it. We're gonna make it.' It was literally like we were waiting to cross some threshold or border to safety."

Repeatedly, respondents explained that they did not expect the license issuing to last. They feared an injunction at any moment and felt no respite until their license was officially registered with the City of San Francisco, even running through the courthouse to complete the process. Brian, the lawyer, described his fears as he and Robert waited in line: "There was something that was going to happen. There was going to be the big announcement on the PA system: 'It's all done. Stop.' Nothing that dramatic, but, you know—that there would be some court order and the injunction would be granted and then there would be an announcement and we'd have to stop." More succinctly, Robert, the physical therapist, stated, "The main anxiety was we're not going to get—it's not going to happen." They worried that they would not have the opportunity to legally marry.

The nearly desperate urgency some participants felt as they waited in line around city hall is a far cry from the emotions generally associated with weddings. Instead, it points to the extent to which participants believed—even expected—that they would be excluded from marriage, just as gays and lesbians have historically been excluded from state-sanctioned marriage and other social rights. This learned acceptance of exclusion, in the narratives of several respondents, began at the same time they embraced their homosexuality. Respondents commented that the experience of embracing a homosexual identity also meant changing their expectations of life and the world. Marriage was off the table once you came out.

The normative expectation that everyone should marry, however, did not go away, meaning that gays and lesbians were constantly reminded of their non-normative status. Olivia, the programmer, described this double-bind of social pressure to marry and the exclusion of gay and lesbian couples from marriage, saying, "Marriage is something that our society tells you you're supposed to want. From day one, what you're supposed to do is grow up and get married. Maybe not immediately, but eventually: you're supposed to grow up and get married and have kids. So, they feed you this for years and years and years and then you find out, well, it's not for us. . . . Marriage meant marriage to a man. I really couldn't see that, you know? So I was rather incensed that society would say, on the one hand, 'This is what you're supposed to do.' And then say, 'Oh, but not you.'" Just as many participants spoke of believing marriage was out of reach because they had come out as gay, other scholars have found similar perceptions by out gays and lesbians about their access to the broader construct of "family" (Weston 1991). Early writings on homosexuality often accepted the equation between being gay and exclusion from family (for example, Altman 1979; Berzon 1979). For many lesbians and gays, at least initially, embracing a homosexual identity was associated with disavowing a future that holds marriage and family.

This belief that marriage was simply unavailable was so strongly held that even as they cautiously waited in line, some respondents reported feeling like they were doing something they were not supposed to. Lois, the physical therapist, for example, described feeling like she was trespassing or borrowing without permission: "It was really pretty intense and weird and like trying on somebody else's jeans and liking them on you, but it's not quite you. . . . A lot of real weird—intense and wonderful, yet weird—feelings about that. It was really intense." Diana, the administrative assistant, noted that everyone was on their best behavior, hoping to be deemed worthy of this opportunity. As she described it, "Everybody was very, very civil. Everybody was very calm and still very happy. We passed the word that we're not going to be upset about how long it's taking. We didn't want to upset anybody. It was like being children, not wanting to upset the apple cart. Just keep going, keep going, keep your fingers crossed, and hopefully we'll inch our way all the way through those double doors to get our licenses." Lois, Diana, and others remembered being concerned that their newfound feeling of inclusion would be withdrawn. As Phoebe phrased it, "It started out as an 'I can't believe this is happening' and then became 'let's get up there and get it done before they stop it.'" This fear illustrates just how foreign this opportunity for marriage was for many participants and how embedded their assumption that they would be excluded. They worried that something too good to be true perhaps was.

As the nervousness waned, respondents noted increasing feelings of inclusion and disbelief, often felt simultaneously. They voiced again and again their pleasure and surprise that San Francisco decided to issue them a wedding license. In their experience of receiving a license, participants like Keith, the lawyer, reported feeling an unexpectedly relieving feeling of equality and inclusion. Keith explained, "There was this electric chill physically and transformation within as well as without with the legal document. It was the sense of feeling, for the first time, that we're actually fully equal in the eyes of the law and the government, something we'd never imaged that we ever could possibly do." Anne, the artist, also remarked on the potent feeling of inclusion she experienced during the San Francisco weddings. She said, "It's a really different experience. It's a really different thing. It was very different to be able to finally do that. It was great. I would've done it a hundred times just 'cause it was so fun. It was so completing for us, finally." The feeling was sometimes sparked by the most simple of gestures. For Craig, the research manager, it was the forms: "The forms were the same forms that everybody else was using—[that] was exhilarating. It's like, damn, it's about time."

In these reported emotions, interviewees implicitly cited previous feelings of *exclusion*, largely owing to their sexual identity. This feeling of inclusion was a feeling of success, of accomplishment through the legalization of gay and lesbian marriage. Participants described their pleasure in being able to be fully "themselves" through their participation in legal marriage and to be able, at last, to relax a little in the safety of inclusion. Lynn, the senior center director, said, "Being a lesbian and being in a committed relationship is a revolutionary act. It's a daily revolutionary act. It's a big deal. It's like we're just being ourselves and it's really a big deal. So to have that support, to feel that when you're coming in or going out to get married was really amazing. It really meant a lot to me." As we spoke, Lynn gestured widely as she described how it felt to marry in city hall and her voice grew louder as she said, "I felt so excited. It was one of the most exciting times of my life, and I felt my energy as big as the building—the energy just going straight up. I was in my body, but I felt like my body was huge or something. It was this amazing feeling of just being totally exhilarated in a way that I have not felt that often in my life." For Lynn and others, feeling the government support them enabled them to fully feel empowered to pursue their desires.

That feeling could be overwhelming. Sonia, the public employee, explained, "In a lot of ways I was also struck by the historical aspect of this, which also made me very humble. To be one of the few, that was very, very humbling." Sonia is African American and parts of her experience reminded her of the history of civil rights activism. She related, "Matter of fact, in one of the rotundas they had some kind of display and it had something to do with segregation in the South. . . . I just stood still for a moment and just kind of looked around at all the other people and all that was going on: men and men, women and women, all ethnic groups, all racial groups, all combinations. I can't say that I have ever experienced some of those things, some of those feelings at that depth. It just stopped me dead in my tracks. I was so full that I wanted to cry and couldn't cry and it was just amazing, just amazing." Participants' charged emotional responses point to the lifting of a burden and a feeling of increased acceptance and freedom. Legal marriage, for these respondents, eliminated an affront to their dignity and the question of their legitimacy as members of society, allowing them increased feelings of freedom.

These feelings surfaced even for respondents who actively disavowed an interest in marriage. Terrance, as we've seen, did not think he or his relationship needed marriage, but he surprised himself in having a positive emotional experience of his wedding. He felt good about his marriage because the experience was one of inclusion. As he put it, "The grace and the dignity that was given to it all was just—words can't express that feeling. It felt complete. And how odd to say it felt complete for someone who would've said, no, I don't really need marriage to make my relationship complete. But yeah, there was a sense of, oh, this is how it feels." Terrance's wedding signaled a larger acceptance, even encouragement, for his relationship. He did not explicitly need it, but he appreciated it nonetheless.

Overcoming Shame

The experience of legal marriage allowed some respondents to shed not just the experience of exclusion, but some internally held shame. Despite taking active measures to eliminate feelings of second-class status, lesbians and gays cannot help but be influenced by heteronormative society. Standing in the city hall rotunda, Keith was surprised to discover still-held shame over being gay and pleased that access to marriage helped dispel it. He said, "It really was very illuminating to see how much that stuff [shame] still is held. . . . I never thought I would get to do this; that's for someone else. It embedded something in me that I was always going to be less than equal, never going to be fully accepted. That all shed when Tim and I legally married. Of course, emotional changes don't occur instantly, but we had the taste, we had the feeling: wow, we're fully equal and we don't carry shame with us." Keith's comment exemplifies how some respondents explained their emotions of inclusion and disbelief by couching them in their previously held self-perception of being fully out as gay.

Ellen Riggle and Sharon Rostosky (2007) have argued that gays and lesbians experience "minority stress," a type of chronic stress experienced by stigmatized groups that leads to negative health outcomes. In this model, because of the ongoing experience of prejudice against sexual minorities, gays and lesbians report lower levels of life satisfaction (Garnets and Kimmel 1993; Lane and Wegner 1995; Savin-Williams and Rodriguez 1993) and higher levels of stress-sensitive mental health problems (Mays and Cochran 2001). Moreover, the experience of minority stress can lead to internalized homophobia and feelings of shame. Riggle and Rostosky (2007) argue that legal same-sex marriage can alleviate minority stress, a claim borne out by the experience of respondents like Keith.

Social movement scholars would suggest a different cause for this emotional shift. Lory Britt and David Heise (2000), for instance, point to the importance of participation in collective events for transforming sexual identity–based shame into pride. Similarly, Verta Taylor and Nancy Whittier (1995) identify such emotional shifts as a central goal of the women's movement. The San Francisco weddings were clearly collective events, and this collectivity—rather than the receipt of a legal marriage license—may have been the catalyst for some respondents overcoming embedded feelings of shame.

Nervous, anxious, excited, and cautious, respondents reported another emotion that must be understood as unique to the gay and lesbian experience of marriage and, perhaps, too, to the San Francisco circumstances: the feeling of safety. Kelly, the professor, quietly said in her interview, "It felt so safe there." Keith's comment went into greater depth: "It was still so wonderful to know that, in my city hall, my city, and my county, that I could go and be safe in my own government. Know that love and commitment and responsibility to people were being nurtured. It was profound."

For Ernesto, the health educator, this feeling of safety underscored the ongoing lived difference between his life and that of straight people. Despite his insistence that he married Tony for the same reasons as heterosexual couples marry, he paused when asked about how his experience might differ from theirs and offered an explanation that identifies the normalization of heterosexual privilege. He said, "It was just a thrill to be sitting there where everybody's gay and everybody's there with the same purpose. Well, maybe not everybody's gay, some people that were working there most likely not, but they were certainly gay positive. . . . And I thought, hmm, this is what straight people experience every day of their life. I had never experienced this before. It was very energizing. . . . it was a feeling of well-being, amazing well-being." Although Ernesto characterized San Francisco as a very gay-friendly place, he was nonetheless struck by the extent to which he felt supported in city hall. Noting that difference, how there was still a gap between his everyday experience of inclusion and what he surmised is a typical straight experience, was emotionally powerful for Ernesto.

These emotions of safety, inclusion, and well-being demand to be contextualized in the history of discrimination against lesbians and gays. They also point to the power of the institution of marriage. For many, the experience of legal marriage, paired with their lived experience in a heteronormative society, was cathartic. Deirdre, the writer, volunteered on several different days at city hall as well as getting married herself. She explained why she was drawn back to the events again and again, saying, "There were so many tears at city hall. We're talking about people who've been rejected or judged all their lives. . . . There were people who never felt safe holding hands with their life partners. There were people who have been judged and scoffed at by their children's educators. The experience for them of being validated by a governmental body, by authority when authority has often been the source of their pain, it brought so many people to tears, and I could see the healing beginning."

By Deirdre's account, it was not just that these individuals had the opportunity to marry, it was that they felt included by the very institution that had excluded them before. They had the opportunity to see how much they had internalized homophobia. Deirdre continued, "In the community, I just see the marks of so much self-destruction that I think is symptomatic of living in a homophobic culture. This was the opposite of a homophobic culture. This was—we're embracing and celebrating you and excited about you and interested in you and we're giving you things for free because you're gay [laughs]. There were so many people that have never had that experience before, and that's what I mean by healing. It's an opportunity for some healing to begin, even if it's just to open the floodgates of grief about past pain." Deirdre wanted to be a witness to that healing and support its continuation in any way she could. In addition to volunteering many days at city hall, Deirdre collected the stories of many people who were married and sought to publish them as a testimony of the Winter of Love.

As many participants acknowledged, lesbian and gay individuals in contemporary society experience systematic homophobia, from external forces and sometimes from within. For many respondents, the experience of coming out meant accepting a different life course than they were raised to expect, a life course that would not include marriage and family. As much as many of the individuals I interviewed embraced a gay or lesbian identity, the surprising experience of legal marriage engendered feelings that reminded them of the often hidden wounds they had experienced and the protective gear they had donned.

Adding Insult to Injury

Respondents' reactions to the California Supreme Court's ruling in August of 2004 further highlight how the overall experience helped expose the pervasiveness of heterosexual privilege. In part, this occurred because the marriage invalidation again showed the gap between the normative "marriage story" and same-sex couples' experience. Some respondents experienced that ruling as painful. Anne cried as she remembered how she felt when she learned of the court's decision. Their ruling that the marriages were invalid because the mayor had overstepped his jurisdiction was devastating to her. Her wife, Lynn, explained, "When the court decided that we were not legally married, Anne called me at work. She was crying. I said, 'What's the matter?' She goes, 'We're not legally married anymore.' She was crying. It was so sad."

Over time, Anne had committed to the belief that the marriages were legal—she allowed herself to feel normative. She was hurt when the ruling was announced, but that pain issued not only from the court's decision. It also came from her recognition that the ruling was made *because* those who wedded were not straight. She saw the decision as evidence of how different-sex couples are treated differently from same-sex couples. And it was not just that gays and lesbians couldn't marry, it was that they could marry, believe they were legally married, and then have it taken away. Such a scenario would never happen to a different-sex couple. Through tears, she said,

> Imagine if they took all the straight people and said, "You're not married anymore." Imagine if they just did that to people, just said, "You're not married anymore. Your marriage is voided because of some stupid ass court thing." It's the stupidest thing you can imagine if they just took, let's take Connecticut, and said, "Oops, sorry, you're not married anymore. We made a mistake. You're not allowed to get married. Your marriage is now void. Your kids are

not your kids anymore. You don't own your house together. All the legal things you've been enjoying are no longer in place. You can't file your taxes together. You can't do any of that stuff." Nobody can take it away from them, but they can take it away from us. They can say, "Oops, sorry. It's not good anymore. Your marriage is void. You're instantly annulled for no reason." It just doesn't make sense.

Anne believed all couples should be treated equally. The court's decision showed her that she and Lynn were not being treated as a different-sex couple would be and exposed the ongoing operation of heterosexual privilege.

Dale, the nightclub manager, felt the ruling sharply as well, even as he admitted that he never genuinely believed the marriages would hold. As did Anne, Dale cried as he remembered hearing about the court's ruling. He said, "Yeah, we knew [the invalidation] was going to happen, but until they actually said it, it didn't seem real. That's what hurt so much." Dale felt that the court did more than it had to in deciding to void the licenses and that is what really stung. He said, "What they did is they took an extra step and they actually annulled our weddings. They annulled. They didn't have to do that. That wasn't why they were there. They actually went one step further than they had to. It should have been completely, separately decided, but they went out of their way to go ahead and say, 'No, they're null and void.' That's kind of what made it so rough that day. I wasn't expecting that to happen. I was expecting them to say that it wasn't legal and I was fine with that. But for them to also go that way and to say that they were null and void? That's what was upsetting." We could say that Dale experienced the court's decision as one that added insult to (hidden) injury. He had already accepted the fact that the weddings were likely to be ruled invalid—tacitly accepting socialized exclusion from marriage—but he was surprised by a ruling he interpreted to say he never had been married, thus expanding the scope of his anticipated exclusion. Heteronormativity was bigger than he thought—and he thought he knew how far it reached.

The ruling left some respondents feeling powerless in the face of heteronormativity. Frank, with fifty years of commitment to Henry, said the ruling pushed him "into a blue funk for a long time." Others felt anger and frustration when they learned that their marriage license had been voided. Phoebe explained that she was "livid." She pointedly felt that the invalidation ruling was personal. She experienced the court's decision as discounting her humanity by denying her something available to others: "I completely felt like I didn't matter, that who I was was not as important as the person who lived next door to me or the person in the grocery store line with me."

For Phoebe, it was not just that the courts ruled that the marriages were no longer valid, it was their ruling that they never were legal in the first place that made her so angry. She fumed, "They ruled them null and void from inception, meaning that they had never taken place. They didn't simply just invalidate them. Had they invalidated them, then for six months, I would've been married. But they didn't do it that way. They ruled them void from inception, meaning they had not taken place at all." She felt their ruling erased her experience. That beautiful day she had and the incredible emotional bump she received from being married was pulled out from under her: "And it sort of just said that everything that happened—the flowers being sent across the country, the news coverage, all those people standing in line in the rain, people bringing them food—saying that all that didn't happen. It was very frustrating." All this emphasized to Phoebe her marginal status as a lesbian and reminded her that she lived in a world of heterosexual privilege. Not only could she be denied privileges afforded others, she could be given them and then have them taken away.

Robert called the voiding "ridiculous," and Brian, whose training as a lawyer helped him follow the case closely, considered that part of the decision "extraordinary." Brian believed the court was able to preserve those marriages even as they sanctioned the mayor. Although intellectually they debated the merits of the case, they could not escape its emotional impacts as well: both also called the decision "upsetting."

Like the emotions respondents reported experiencing during their city hall ceremonies, the feelings the Supreme Court of California engendered when it ruled the licenses invalid illustrate the unique positionality of lesbians and gays in contemporary society. The decision hit some respondents viscerally; it hurt them. That hurt came from the reminder, in the form of the decision, that their relationship was less valued than a different-sex relationship. Perhaps more importantly, that hurt came after many respondents had begun feeling a sense of belonging. Having months of legal marriage, respondents became accustomed to their status and gingerly allowed themselves to feel normative, illustrating the tremendous appeal of accepting normative status. They experienced the court decision as a reminder of their marginalized status, seen ever more starkly from the vantage of their brief experience of (partial) normativity.

Missing from respondents' accounts of their reactions to the license invalidation were stories of how their return to non-married status affected their relationship. Indeed, being un-married appeared to matter in respondents' accounts almost exclusively for their thinking about the public aspect of marriage, not in their private lives. The changes marriage enacted in respondents' personal lives, including within their relationships and in their interactions with others, persisted. Invalidating the licenses did not make in-laws and coworkers revert to treating the couples as not committed. Respondents may have noticed the long reach of heterosexual privilege when their marriages were invalidated, but the subtle impacts on their lives of the normative status of married largely remained invisible.

Unmarried and Mobilized

No longer married, many respondents decided to do something about their marginalized status. For most, same-sex marriage was not on their radar prior to the Winter of Love. Even after the contentious battle over the Knight Initiative in 2000, which added a defense of marriage act to California law, marriage equality did not rank high among the issues they were prepared to advocate about. Some admitted that they never really thought about marriage before the 2004 weddings. But those hours in line, those vows they spoke in city hall, and that social support they experienced throughout the process and in the months afterwards changed their prioritization of marriage equality.[1] Now, it was important.

This was definitely true for Robert. His city hall wedding and the marriage that ensued changed his thinking about marriage equality as a cause. He said, "I'm more confident since we married and sure of the fact that it should be legal. It should be the law. Before it was,

'Yeah, but I don't know.' We weren't committed to it. Now, the idea of it, we're committed to." His partner, Brian, also described a shift in his thinking. Before the marriages, Brian thought the legal benefits were what really mattered, regardless of the package they came in. Now, he wants marriage. He initially wondered "if it [marriage] was necessary. I thought we could make do with civil unions. That was our position. I was prepared to accept that before. Not now." He was willing to do more than simply pay lip service to his desire for marriage. He was ready to mobilize. He stated, "I feel very strongly about it. If that's the definition of an activist, then we're definitely there. I know we're giving more money. I feel like we're—I can't put it in concrete terms—I feel like we're more activists now than we were before." Not only did their experience in the San Francisco weddings change how respondents thought about marriage, it changed how they thought about their role in campaigns for social change.

Marrying served as a wake-up call for Phoebe, the analyst, jolting her out of her everyday concerns. She said, "It helped me realize that I needed to do more than just live day to day. I needed to get involved. I needed to do more activism type things." Her experience in marriage taught her how important it was to her to be recognized as a family and to have access to the legal protections of marriage. It also taught her that such hopes were possible, if she and others were willing to put in some effort. She said, "[My marriage] helped me see that there are people out there that are supportive of my relationship and we should do more to make those relationships visible." Experiencing the collectivity at city hall and the encouragement of people in all facets of her life, gay and straight alike, persuaded Phoebe that marriage equality was possible.

When she returned home after her San Francisco wedding, Phoebe channeled her energy into the movement, hosting webpages for advocacy groups, volunteering regularly at the local LGBT center, sponsoring a booth on marriage at her local Pride event, and holding yard sales with proceeds benefiting local marriage equality organizations. In her mind, her marriage and her activism were linked. Her ability to marry reminded her that others had paved the road for her, and this inspired her to work for those who would come after. She explained, "I would not have gotten involved in a lot of these things had it not been for the support of the folks before me. Seeing the people that went ahead, the pioneers of the movement, who were getting the door slammed in their face just so I could stand in line and get married. It made me realize I had a responsibility to those who were coming up after me. I have to get out and get involved and get the word out and make it where seeing a same-sex couple get married isn't the end of the world." Whereas, before the weddings, Phoebe had only visited a few advocacy websites, after the weddings, she spent several hours a day communicating with others on behalf of marriage equality and other queer rights issues.

Sophie told a similar story of increasing her activism, but her methods were more personal. After the weddings, in addition to coalition building with a number of groups she participates in, Sophie made a concerted choice with her partner, Lal, to be more out about their non-normative family. Sophie considers this a form of activism, demonstrating the validity of their lives, and they have taken it to new heights.

> Our daughter's first birthday was the day after [Arnold] Schwarzenegger vetoed the same-sex marriage bill here. And somebody had called to see if we wanted to speak to the media. And I was, like, "I'm running around trying to get food and party hats and stuff for my daughter's first birthday." They were like, "First birthday? [Can we attend as members of the media?]" It was this, this momentous thing in our family and it's also a very private thing. We kind of struggled with it a little bit. But we did it. The local television station came out and documented her first birthday as part of our response to how his veto affected our communities.

Sophie saw this as a new kind of engagement in activism for queer families. She said, "I don't think we would've done that before we got married. I don't think that we would've thought that our voices mattered that much." The marriages encouraged Sophie and Lal to make a claim for their right to be seen as a family.

Others were mobilized in different ways, participating in marches, writing letters, calling elected officials. Across respondents, two-thirds reported that the marriages increased their level of activism, predominantly on the marriage equality issue (see also Taylor et al. 2009).

The marriages and their subsequent invalidation impacted not only individuals and families, but the community. Deirdre saw incredible possibilities for mobilization for social change stemming from the marriages. She explained, "I think that it's an experience that has empowered so many people—and frustrated a lot of people, which can be empowering, too—because then that kicks you into action. I think that the beauty of it was what it did to inspire and heal people and get people to expect more for themselves and get frustrated and do something. That was the lasting impression for me."

No matter what, those experiences of marriage were not going to go away. Raine, the disabled retiree, said, despite any homophobic claims opponents may make, "They can't take the experience away. My name is still on that piece of paper and so is Isabel's and so is our witness. They can't take that. They can never take that away." Sophie saw that experience of inclusion as potent. She said, "It was a very different movement before we had those pieces of paper in our hands, and they can't take that back. We have a really different perspective now. I don't know anybody that went through the experience that wasn't changed." The San Francisco weddings changed their participants, showed them how marriage operates to perpetuate heterosexual privilege. They learned, from the inside, what marriage could mean and what it felt like to be a part of that privileged status.

Beyond the Gay and Lesbian Community

Respondents were disappointed that the marriages were invalidated, but many hopefully suggested that not all was lost. Some optimistically posited positive impacts of the marriages on society at large, even after the licenses were voided, arguing that the marriages exposed the inequality of denying same-sex couples access to marriage. Philip, who considered his earlier commitment ceremony his real wedding, explained that the marriages showed the importance of marriage to same-sex couples. He said, "I think they were more testaments to how important marriage is to people. It showed people in San Francisco— even though everyone is more open to gays and lesbians already—and it showed the world that there are a lot of people that are gay and lesbian who want to get married. The news was around the world, so it really showed that things need to change. I think it really elevated the issue to the national level." Similarly, Laura, the disabled retiree, believed the visibility of the weddings did much to forward the marriage rights cause as a social justice issue, highlighting discrimination against lesbian and gay couples: "And because of all the publicity and things, I think it actually changed more people in favor of than against. Some people who were against have changed, but I don't think it did the other way with people who were for it because they saw what it meant to people." Elizabeth, the accounting assistant, went a bit further, suggesting that the marriages' impact on social consciousness was significant enough to make it almost OK that the marriages did not last. She said, "It almost—almost—doesn't matter if it's legal or not. Everybody's talking about it because it's on the news. People at work were talking about it. People on the bus were talking about it. Everybody was talking about it. And I thought, this is great, because five years before that, or even less, it wasn't really on the horizon for most people. It was a dream in a few people's heads." The city hall weddings forced the issue of same-sex marriage onto the national stage and made people confront the fact that marriage is reserved for different-sex couples.

Ernesto, the health educator, explained, "[The marriages] put a human face on a gay issue. And that's important. It has an impact. We are making people aware of injustice." It started a movement. As Raine put it, "I think a lot of people that were asleep about it woke up, and some people that couldn't have cared less started to care. A lot of people, like a friend of mine, became activists for us (and several became activists against us). It was just a very, a defining moment for sure that can't be ignored. Some of the other [gay rights] things that happened were just, you know, like little temper tantrums. This wasn't. This was a movement." Raine's claim is borne out. In the years following the San Francisco events, a coherent marriage equality movement has emerged.

Arguably, the San Francisco events catalyzed this same-sex marriage movement in California and fed the fire of activism throughout the United States. They had the immediate effect of spawning a series of similar executive decisions to recognize same-sex unions across the country. On February 28, 2004, eight days after San Francisco began issuing marriage licenses to gay and lesbian couples, a clerk in Sandoval, New Mexico, issued a handful of licenses to same-sex couples. The mayor of New Paltz, New York, married twenty-five same-sex couples on February 27. A few days later, on March 3, Multnomah County, Oregon, began issuing marriage licenses to same-sex couples. Over 3,000 such licenses were issued before April 20, when a judge in the Multnomah County Circuit Court ordered the county to cease issuing such licenses, while simultaneously ordering the state of Oregon to recognize the 3,022 licenses already issued. All these events were just a prelude to legal same-sex marriage in Massachusetts, which began May 18, 2004, and remains legal, unlike the other examples described here.

In California, the San Francisco marriages set into motion a series of lawsuits both in opposition to the weddings and, when the marriages were ruled invalid in August 2004, in support of lesbian and gay couples' right to marry. This second set of cases made it to the California Supreme Court, which ruled in May 2008 that it is unconstitutional in California to bar gay and lesbian couples from marrying. In June of that year, same-sex couples in California were legally allowed to marry. Over eighteen thousand couples did until, five months later, in November 2008, California voters approved Proposition 8, a constitutional amendment that returned marriage exclusively to different-sex couples. The constitutionality of Proposition 8 was then challenged in federal court. In August of 2010, a federal circuit judge ruled that Proposition 8 was unconstitutional. State officials declined to appeal the ruling, but private entities assumed this task, appealing up to the US Supreme Court. In June 2013, the high court ruled that these private parties lacked standing to appeal, effectively reinstating the original ruling and paving the way for same-sex marriage to resume in California. Within days, San Francisco's city hall was, once again, issuing marriage licenses to same-sex couples. And the national story continues. As Isabel, the professor, said, "You can't put the genie back in the bottle."

Although the Winter of Love weddings did not remain valid, respondents believed their marriage experiences introduced the possibility of same-sex marriage to the public. Ernesto explained, "There's always a sense of possibility: it happened before [and] it will happen again. It's not it *can* happen again, but it *will* happen again." And with

that possibility, the otherwise unrecognized construction of heterosexual privilege through marriage had to be noticed.

If nothing else, the marriages gave respondents an opportunity to
talk about their exclusion from marriage as part of sexual identity–based
inequality. For instance, Tim, the policy analyst, used his marriage to
educate gay-friendly coworkers about the inequality he experienced as a
member of a same-sex couple. One progressive colleague, in particular,
expressed surprise that he chose that day—a Thursday—to get married.
Tim related his experience, "This one woman came into my office later
after some of the conversations had died down and she said, 'So, how
did you choose today to get married?' I said, 'Um, because it was illegal
yesterday.' She was actually surprised to know that. Obviously, she was
not informed on this issue." Tim considered the interaction further and
suggested that his colleague probably believed that he should have full
equality but had not thought through the ways in which Tim did not.
As long as she was unaware of marriage discrimination—not to mention other manifestations of inequality—she was unlikely to be an ally
in efforts to change it.

Other respondents used similar interactions with supportive
friends and colleagues to push beyond simple questions of marriage
equality to discuss the social valuation of heterosexuality over alternative sexualities. For example, Terrance recalled the support his straight
friends offered after his wedding, noting that it was somewhat mis-
placed. He said, "Our heterosexual friends thought that we needed
state sanction. Our neighbors said, 'Oh, well, that's good for you guys.
Now you're like us.' [I replied,] 'No, we aren't like you, and here's why.'
It gave us a platform to say, 'No, we aren't like you and these are the
reasons why.'" Terrance appreciated that the weddings offered him
the opportunity to talk about heterosexual privilege and articulate
how gays and lesbians are marginalized, not simply because same-sex
couples are denied marriage licenses. The marriages became part of a
larger movement of exposing heteronormativity.

No Longer an Imaginary Heterosexual Privilege

In the years since the San Francisco weddings, we have not witnessed
a dramatic overhaul of the meaning of marriage. Heteronormativity is

still firmly in place and remains closely implicated in the institution of marriage. But discourse around same-sex marriage has shifted nonetheless. Opinion polls show increasing acceptance of same-sex marriage, and several more states have joined Massachusetts in offering marriage licenses to same-sex couples. Change has not come easily, but there are hints that its incremental progress will continue.

This increasing awareness of the issue of marriage equality owes to the movement, and the movement has clear roots in the San Francisco weddings. They helped put the issue of same-sex marriage on the map. In more subtle ways, the city hall weddings drew respondents' attention to the ongoing operation of heteronormativity in their lives. Through the weddings, heterosexual privilege was exposed—not just in terms of access to marriage, but in terms of the psychological experience of being a sexual minority in contemporary society, even in the gay-friendly Bay Area. As Ernesto and Tim recognized, straight people have the privilege of going through life expecting inclusion in government, safety, and a life without shame over their sexual identity. The accounts of my respondents show how this is not the case for many gays and lesbians. The marriages brought visceral evidence of the social marginalization of lesbians and gays to the debate on same-sex marriage.

As respondents were attuned to how access to marriage is a heterosexual privilege, many, in turn, devoted themselves to communicating about that privilege in the hopes of creating social change. In theoretical terms, the marriages offered respondents the opportunity to bring the heterosexual imaginary (Ingraham 1994) into focus. At least in part, heterosexual privilege could not be ignored; it had to be acknowledged. And in acknowledgment, some of heteronormativity's hegemony is necessarily undone. If heteronormativity's strength owes in part to its invisibility, bringing it to light unmakes it at least in part. What happens next depends on what people decide to do about the no longer imaginary—or, perhaps, less imaginary—heterosexual.

CHAPTER 8

CONCLUSION

The San Francisco weddings were a sight to behold. Happy couples lined up in inclement weather, wearing trash bags from generous supporters to keep their clothes dry; passing cars honked their horns loudly; cheers erupted and bubbles floated through the air as same-sex couples exited city hall, registered marriage license in hand. Nothing quite like this had ever happened before. As person after person I interviewed recounted their wedding, the joy of those experiences was palpable. They showed me photos and news clippings, presented me with copies of their marriage certificates, and shared intimate emotions with me in their interviews. I was transfixed by the excitement and happiness of those events as they unfolded and even more so as I interviewed men and women who married. Listening to their interviews years later and retelling their stories is a pleasure.

Many of the women and men I spoke with articulated their hope that the San Francisco events would be the start of something big, but none anticipated that so much change around marriage equality would happen in such a short period of time. By February 2013, nine years after the San Francisco weddings, nine states and the District of Columbia offered marriage licenses to same-sex couples. And that number is predicted to continue to grow. What was initially a far-off idea has gained mainstream traction. The San Francisco weddings presaged a new national focus on marriage equality, in which lesbian and gay couples began to make meaning of marriage, seeking to understand not only the institution but their experience of it as well.

As the campaign for same-sex marriage has unfolded, in politics and in popular culture, we can find echoes of the themes initially sounded in the 2004 San Francisco marriages. For one, the social movement for same-sex marriage is not comprised of gays and lesbians alone. Just as the San Francisco events depended on the supportive labor of allies in the straight community, from city hall workers to Mayor Gavin Newsom, heterosexual champions have been instrumental in marriage equality victories. In 2011, in New York state, for instance, newly elected—and heterosexual—governor Andrew Cuomo made marriage equality a primary goal of his early months in office. Less than two years earlier, the legislature had definitively voted against a measure that would have legalized same-sex marriage in New York, and the prospect of a different outcome under Cuomo was uncertain. Undeterred, Governor Cuomo lobbied heavily for the marriage equality act. On June 24, 2011, the New York state legislature passed the same-sex marriage bill. Cuomo signed it into law that very day.

Governor Cuomo was not the only straight, elected official in New York to vociferously endorse same-sex marriage. New York City mayor Michael Bloomberg also lent his support to the issue. Although Bloomberg had no direct voting rights on the issue before the state legislature, he spoke publicly in favor of the measure, both from a personal standpoint and as mayor. Bloomberg described the marriage equality cause as an issue of fairness, saying he was tired of explaining to gay and lesbian friends why they were not permitted to marry. He likened marriage equality to civil rights, women's rights, and workers' rights and asserted that excluding same-sex couples from marriage amounted to unjustified inequality. In identifying marriage as a question of fairness, Bloomberg acknowledged the unequal treatment of lesbian and gay couples and implicitly cited the existence of heterosexual privilege. For respondents like Tim and Keith, incensed at the invisibility they felt when they had to claim "single" status on their tax returns despite nearly two decades together, this was a big victory. Tim and Keith would likely have been pleased to hear a public official recognize that they are discriminated against by being denied access to legal marriage. This sort of public acknowledgement of heterosexual privilege can make significant inroads in dismantling discrimination against lesbian and gay couples.

Bloomberg's explanation of his support for marriage equality coupled this framing with another idea some respondents' offered: the assertion that same-sex couples are just like different-sex couples. Same-sex couples, he asserted, should be allowed to enter into a contract with each other just as different-sex couples are—and that contract is marriage. As respondents Pierre and Addy separately insisted, marriage is about love, and gay couples love each other just like straight couples do. The "same as" claim, like the unequal treatment claim, appears to have achieved resonance beyond the experiences of participants in the San Francisco weddings. As I have noted, however, this claim papers over the ways in which same-sex couples are actually different from different-sex couples, in their needs and in their lived experience. Without attention to the hidden injury of homophobia, the acknowledgment of heterosexual privilege in marriage is unlikely to make much headway in dismantling heteronormativity.

We also have evidence that same-sex marriage has helped bring visibility to lesbian and gay couples, as respondents like Craig hoped it would. For example, when same-sex marriage was legal in California in 2008 (before it was once again made illegal through Proposition 8), talk show host Ellen DeGeneres and actress Portia de Rossi married. DeGeneres announced their engagement on her talk show and the two shared photos of their nuptials in *People* magazine. Although DeGeneres had been publicly out as gay for over a decade and the celebrities' four-year relationship was not a secret, it took marriage to make their (lesbian) relationship the topic of positive mainstream press coverage. Through marriage, DeGeneres's lesbian identity was explicitly acknowledged on her show and in the press.

It is worth noting—just as Terrance and Kelly remarked that the San Francisco marriages enabled "normal"-looking lesbians and gays to gain visibility—that press coverage focused on the more normative aspects of DeGeneres and de Rossi's relationship, such as the home they share with their three dogs and four cats. The narrative of DeGeneres and de Rossi's wedding, in other words, was one of normativity, suggesting that they are no threat to marriage and, by implication, no threat to heteronormativity.

Finally, sounding another theme from my data, there is evidence that marriage is increasingly seen as normative for lesbian and gay couples. In July 2011, the *New York Times* ran an article entitled "Ready to Wed? No, Mom" about the pressure to marry that gays and lesbians in committed relationships are now feeling from parents and friends (T. Murphy 2011). Young gay men and women reported that marriage now seemed like an expected next step. Unlike in 2004, same-sex marriage is now a regular part of social and political discourses.

The Persistence of Heteronormativity

It is not clear that the respondents who wanted their participation to change marriage had the current mainstream vision of same-sex marriage in mind. Barbara, for one, almost certainly would not accept this version of same-sex marriage as evidence of victory. Committed to socialist principles, Barbara explicitly wanted the institution of marriage to change. She wanted its power to codify the transference of power and wealth to be undone and its ability to dispense privilege to be dismantled. Barbara wanted marriage to be a relationship, not a status. Less radically, respondents like Deirdre wanted marriage changed so that a greater number of people were treated equally, including same-sex couples along with different-sex couples in the institution. Deirdre insisted on her right to marriage as a human being, arguing that she and Leslie should be treated with the dignity other deeply committed couples received. She wanted to eliminate some of the privileges afforded to heterosexuals. The current portrait of same-sex marriage comes closer to Deirdre's hopes than to Barbara's.

While the increasingly commonplace status of same-sex marriage and the assumption of its inevitability register as successes for the marriage equality movement, the verdict on its impact on heteronormativity is less definitive. Some themes from the 2004 marriages have clearly resonated, occurring frequently in discourse around marriage, while others are less common. Largely, framings of same-sex marriage that focus on ways it does not destabilize heteronormativity have been popular, much to Barbara's likely disappointment.

On this question of whether the participation of lesbian and gay couples in marriage has disrupted the dominance of heterosexuality, the short answer is no. While many hope that same-sex marriage will definitively demonstrate that gay and lesbian couples are deserving of equal treatment, history suggests that these hopes are not so easily realized. Over the past several decades, technological advances, political changes, and even diseases have been characterized as the step that will lead to an end to discrimination based on sexual identity, and none has lived up to these optimistic hopes (Franklin 1993). It is unlikely, in other words, that the presence of married lesbian and gay couples will change marriage itself. M. V. Lee Badgett (2009) studied married same-sex couples in the Netherlands and found that their participation in marriage generally did not impact the institution. Same-sex marriage successfully mounted a challenge of the heterosexual imperative of marriage but not heteronormativity as a social structure.

Society remains firmly heteronormative in ways both mundane and exceptional and, as respondents' experiences underscore, is immensely adaptable. It has been notably effective in building discourses that privilege heterosexuality around seemingly neutral phenomena. For example, reproductive technologies were expected to undo the biological requirements of different-sex parents and allow anyone, regardless of sexual identity or marital status, to become a parent. However, as Sarah Franklin (1993) shows, the medical discourses that emerged around reproductive technologies, including the requirement of qualifying diagnoses of individual infertility—a diagnosis that applies at the relationship level to a same-sex couple but does not necessarily apply to the individual members of that couple—wound up reinforcing rather than destabilizing heterosexual privilege. Indeed, even stories parents tell in support of their gay or lesbian children have been shown to privilege heterosexuality (Fields 2001). Heteronormativity is not at risk of going anywhere. And its association with weddings and marriage is particularly tenacious (Ingraham 1999; 2003).

But perhaps the answer to the question of whether same-sex marriage effectively disrupts heteronormativity should be this: not so far—and not everyone wants it to. At the same time as they agitated for marriage to change, some respondents wanted parts of marriage to remain the same. By association, they wanted to preserve some aspects of normative privilege. Isabel, whose experience transformed her personally and helped her feel normal, wanted marriage's social meanings preserved as she and Raine sought to enter the institution. She wanted marriage to be the marker of family and to carry with it social legitimacy. While she and Raine may not have needed it for their relationship, they wanted it for their family. In calling for marriage to be extended to same-sex couples, Isabel and Raine did not call heteronormativity out to the mat; they just wanted access to marriage to be expanded.

Respondents like Addy and Julie took this passivity in the face of heteronormativity even further. In their eyes, marriage was about love and their exclusion from marriage was, largely, an oversight. If the world understood that they were just like different-sex couples, it would realize that same-sex couples should be allowed to marry. It would not be about expanding or adapting the institution, just about including those who already qualify.

When the narratives that accompany same-sex marriage fail to challenge heteronormativity, we should not be surprised by its persistence and the extent to which it reaches into lesbian and gay relationships. Marriage can change gay and lesbian relationships: Lynn reported that marriage reoriented the way she and Anne related to one another, making her feel like her eleven-year relationship was suddenly brand new. Marriage can also change how the outside world interacts with lesbian and gay couples, from institutions like Elizabeth's work place having to extend benefits to Laura as her spouse to Keith's brother-in-law finally recognizing him as such after seventeen years to Isabel's stepdaughter seeing her as a mother. It can also channel how same-sex couples choose to celebrate their commitments, encouraging future versions of couples like Janet and Cynthia to publicly declare their commitment instead of privately committing to each other on a mountaintop in Glacier Park. The existence of legal marriage may even encourage a preference for dyadic relationships over alternatives.

The Appeal of Heteronormativity

By analyzing the meanings for marriage not just for their variety but for variation in who deployed them, this analysis makes a second contribution to understanding the persistence of heteronormativity by illustrating how social location matters. Certain meanings for marriage—meanings that differentially embraced and contested heteronormativity—were more frequently cited by participants with particular biographical experiences. Namely, parents more often talked about marriage in ways that preserved its legal and social meanings, and participants who had exposure to a feminist critique of marriage were likely to proffer a strong political critique of heteronormativity. These biographical experiences accrue to lesbians more than gay men and help us understand not only why more lesbians than gay men married in San Francisco, but the disproportionate representation of lesbian couples given their comparatively lower population in California (Simmons and O'Connell 2003).

This higher rate of lesbian participation must be understood as a consequence of their intersecting gender and sexual identities. Lesbian parents, for example, experience a complex set of experiences and constructions that owe dually to their gender and sexual identity. Their experience of achieving pregnancy (Mamo 2007) and as mothers (Lewin 1993) is distinct from that of single or unmarried heterosexual mothers. Likewise, lesbian-feminism constituted a unique movement (Echols 1989; Taylor and Whittier 1992) that actively drew on its members' identities as lesbians. The subsequent variations in how members of these groups thought about the meaning of marriage and their participation in the San Francisco weddings speak to the importance of conceptualizing heteronormativity as a social structure that differentially affects people in different social locations.

A central finding from my closer examination of how social location mattered to how respondents thought about the practice of same-sex marriage and heteronormativity is just how very appealing normativity is, even—perhaps especially—for those who know the sting of being on the outside. This poses complex questions for efforts to address inequality and challenge the hegemony of heterosexuality. Changing the practice of marriage to include same-sex couples alone will not accomplish these goals.

Transformative Practice

In many ways, this book has grappled with the question, what does same-sex marriage do to heteronormativity? I have suggested that gays and lesbians hoped their marriages would challenge heterosexual privilege and that marriage also changed them. This formulation underemphasizes the importance of practice in understanding same-sex marriage. Marriage is only an institution; it cannot do anything. People *do* things. How they do things and what they say about their actions—how they make meaning of them—are where change is encouraged or blocked.

Marriage is often conceptualized as a deterministic institution. Scholars have written about same-sex marriage in ways that position marriage itself as an entity that would create change (for example, Bernstein 2001; Calhoun 2000; Kandaswamy 2008; Wolfson 2004). Priya Kandaswamy (2008), for example, argues that the institution of marriage is a tool of hegemonic power that punishes non-heteronormative individuals. As had feminists in the decades before her (Auchmuty 2004; Jeffreys 2004), Kandaswamy highlights the institutional power of marriage and wonders about its ability to be remade for alternative meanings. Mary Bernstein (2001), in contrast, posits that the inclusion of same-sex couples in areas circumscribed by family law, including marriage, adoption, and insemination policies, fundamentally challenges hegemonic notions of family. Redefining marriage to include same-sex couples, not the actual participation of gay and lesbian couples in marriage, in the flattest rendering of Bernstein's far more nuanced argument, becomes the act that determines the meaning of marriage.

Marriage, however, is neither monolithic nor deterministic. While the rules about entrance into and exit from marriage have certainly sculpted gender identities, sexual identities, and, indeed, citizenship, in the United States (Cott 2000), the institution itself has been associated with different meanings over time (Coontz 2005). Even without the prospect of same-sex marriage, the meaning of marriage is being transformed by the rise of singlehood, single motherhood, cohabitation, and divorce, as well as by changing negotiations within heterosexual marriages about fertility. Marriage does not organize people's lives in the same way(s) it has in the past (Cherlin 2004). Its meaning has been changed, in other words, by the changing practice of marriage.

To understand the social impact of same-sex marriage, then, we must attend to the practice of marriage, including the narratives of that practice. These narratives are sociological phenomena, not simply abstract texts. At their heart, they are what Ken Plummer (1995) calls "sexual stories." Although not explicitly about sex, these are stories about intimate citizenship, stories that remake definitions of the family, and stories that both cite and disrupt existing discourses. These personal narratives, taken together and contextualized in the prevailing discourses, give us a fuller portrait of the practice of same-sex marriage. Ultimately, it is the practice that gives the institution meaning and leads to the outcomes— transformative or conservative—discussed here.

All of the women and men I spoke with supported marriage equality. We might infer that they therefore implicitly supported an end to inequality based on sexual identity. These are, however, two distinct narratives and, while compatible, one does not necessarily follow from the other. Indeed, they can exist at cross-purposes. Plummer (1995, 176) explains that "[narratives] have conservative, preservative, policing control tasks—as well as transgressive, critical, challenging tasks." It matters whether the practice of same-sex marriage comes with a strong critique of heteronormativity bent on revolutionizing the social order or with a weak critique that is more focused on expanding the boundaries of marriage. The consequences of same-sex marriage for heteronormativity depend on the accounts we give of what marriage means. The disruption of heteronormativity can take place only when (same-sex) marriage is accompanied by an articulated critique of hegemonic heterosexuality. Without a narrative that consciously embraces a challenge of heteronormativity, it is more likely that gays and lesbians will be assimilated into the cultural norm based on heterosexuality than that their participation in marriage will undo heterosexual privilege.

For a goal of undoing heteronormativity—and the gender and sexuality-based inequality associated with it—we must adopt different stories about the way the world works and actively reject narratives that privilege heterosexuality, producing what Michel Foucault (1978) terms a reverse discourse. The second part of this task is paramount. A reverse discourse challenges the stories and meanings of a prevailing discourse, providing a counter-narrative of social processes. Without one, alternative experiences remain exceptional and the normative is preserved.

In the end, the impact of same-sex marriage is not the simple preservation or transgression of heteronormativity. Marriage has both liberatory and assimilationist possibilities. When we pay attention to *how* the practice of same-sex marriage impacts heteronormativity, the complexity of heteronormativity as a social structure is clear. Heteronormativity is nuanced, it is tenacious, and it is appealing. The variation in meanings respondents offered for marriage shows how empirical analyses of gay men's and lesbians' experience of legal marriage complicate linear claims of same-sex marriage's social effect, be they claims of marriage as inherently disruptive of heteronormativity or as automatically reifying heterosexual structures. There is no simple story about what the San Francisco marriages meant to the participants. In looking at the relationship between marriage and heteronormativity, I have illuminated how privilege and inequality are (re)produced as well as some avenues for contesting the marginalization of non-normative sexualities. The practice of marriage is ongoing, tracking shifting meanings for marriage and the experience of being wed. I, for one, am looking forward to observing its evolution.

METHODOLOGICAL
APPENDIX

PARTICIPANT INTERVIEWS

Between May and December of 2006, I interviewed forty-two individuals who were married at city hall during the 2004 events in San Francisco. Interviews were semistructured and ranged in length from forty minutes to two and a half hours, averaging about ninety minutes. All interviews were taped and transcribed for analysis.

RECRUITMENT AND SAMPLING

Respondents were found using snowball sampling. In response to an email sent to personal contacts, my first interview took place in May 2006 and all other interviews flowed from that first one, save for three that were also generated by personal contacts. My request for participants was posted to several listservs by respondents after our interview, including one for Bay Area lesbians, one for East Bay gay and lesbian seniors, one for lesbian and gay parents, and one of contributors to an anthology of personal stories about the weddings. I did not post the request anywhere myself. Although participants were recruited through these postings, they did not necessarily personally know the poster.

Respondents contacted me directly by email and we coordinated a time and place for the interview. Because of my desire to conduct the interviews in person, I scheduled the interviews for times when I would be in the Bay Area (the majority of my respondents lived in the Bay Area, see below, although they were geographically spread out among several counties): May, June, August–September, and December 2006. Over half of the interviews were conducted during my August–September visit. I continued to interview until I reached theoretical saturation.

Timing of Interviews

When I conducted my interviews in 2006, more than two years had passed since the weddings. This gap between the occasion and the interview afforded respondents the opportunity to reflect back on the whole series of events, from their weddings to their marriages to the invalidation. The distance in time was especially useful for capturing how the events did and did not serve to mobilize participants into activism. However, the delay between the weddings and the interviews also creates the possibility of respondents' sentimentalizing their marriages. Retrospective data carries the risk of incomplete memory, which may inaccurately characterize the San Francisco wedding experience. It also makes it difficult to distinguish among effects of the weddings, the marriages, and the invalidation. As I discuss below, interviewing couples together may have ameliorated some tendency to romanticize the past. I also suggest that, keeping the possibility of sentimentalizing in mind, there is still great value in assessing respondents' narratives as they stood in 2006 as testament to the ongoing process of unpacking what the practice of same-sex marriage means to the hegemony of heteronormativity.

Participant Characteristics

My sample included twenty-four women and eighteen men. This breakdown of 57 percent women and 43 percent men mirrors the overall demographics of the population of couples married in San Francisco (see table A.1). These forty-two interviewees represent sixteen lesbian couples and eleven gay men couples. At the time of their 2004 wedding, the interviewees ranged in age from twenty-seven to sixty-eight, with a median age of forty-one. Compared to the demographic data released by the Assessor-Recorder's Office, my interviewees slightly underrepresent the eighteen to thirty-five and the fifty-five to sixty-five age groups and overrepresent the thirty-six to fifty-four and sixty-six and over age groups.

About two-fifths of the respondents in my sample were from San Francisco, representing a diverse range of neighborhoods. This is a higher representation than existed in the population of couples married during the events (Teng 2004). However, my sample was in line with the population's representation of other California locales; 55 percent of the

DEMOGRAPHIC COMPARISON OF RESPONDENTS
AND ASSESSOR-RECORDER'S REPORT

	Assessor-recorder's data* (N = 8,074 total)	Respondents (N = 42 total)**
Gender: % (N)		
Women	57 (4,622)	57 (24)
Men	42 (3,430)	43 (18)
Transgender	—	—
Unknown	0.3 (22)	—
Age: % (N)		
18–35	25.8	21 (9)
36–54	55.4	60 (25)
55–65	17.4	14 (6)
66+	0.9	5 (2)
No age	0.4	—
Education: % (N)		
K–12	11.6	2 (1)
Some college	19	17 (7)
College and higher	68.8	79 (33)
No data	1.6	2 (1)
Geography: % (N)		
California	92	98 (41)
San Francisco	31.65	43 (18)
Oakland	8.51	10 (4)
Sacramento	3.32	0 (0)
Berkeley	2.90	0(0)
Other California	46.38	45 (19)
Other US states & international	8	2 (1)

* The assessor-recorder data reported only percentages for every category save gender. See Teng (2004).

** Numbers do not always sum to 100 percent due to rounding error.

couples in my sample were from other parts of California, mostly the greater Bay Area. According to the city, about 8 percent of the couples married were from outside of California, including residents of all but four of the remaining states in the United States and citizens of eight foreign countries. Only one person I interviewed lived outside of California; he was a resident of Connecticut at the time of the weddings.

The bulk of the weddings took place during the first week that the city issued marriage licenses (Pinello 2006), and my sample reflects that weighting with twenty of the twenty-seven couples represented in my interviews married during the first week. Two couples I interviewed were married the first day, February 12, 2004, and two were married on March 11, the last day licenses were issued. February 13 was the day the largest number of couples represented in my sample married; ten respondent couples were able to receive their marriage licenses that second day.

Key demographics of my respondents are detailed in table A.2. All names are pseudonyms.

On Interviewing Couples

Of the forty-two participants I interviewed, some were interviewed individually and others jointly, all together representing twenty-seven couples. I conducted joint interviews of both members of the couple for fifteen of the couples. I interviewed only one member of the remaining twelve couples. The decision to conduct joint interviews was a conscious one, motivated by the project's goal of teasing out the meanings of marriage to same-sex couples. Joint interviews are useful when a researcher is attempting to understand not just individual accounts but also their context (Morris 2001). They have been found to be particularly effective for inquiries into coupled life (Arksey 1996; Mason 1989; McKee and O'Brien 1983) and have been used specifically to understand meaning-making in marital relationships (Dryden 1999; Porter and Bhattacharya 2008).

Joint interviewing has several benefits, including the opportunity to establish greater rapport and confidence (Edgell 1980). It also had the practical benefit of allowing me to take a smaller role in the interviews themselves, encouraging more elaboration by the respondents. Although joint interviews tended to be longer than solo interviews, my role tended to be substantially smaller. Partners often probed each other's reactions, benefiting from a trust-based relationship more secure than any an interviewer could hope to establish with a newly met interviewee.

Joint interviewing also has the advantage of facilitating the collaborative production of knowledge, allowing one participant to fill in gaps in the memory or knowledge of the other (Seymour et al. 1995; Taylor and Blee 2002). This proved especially valuable in "checking" respondents' reports of their emotional experience of the weddings. For example, in our interview, Lynn challenged Anne's claim that she was happy about the wedding but overall emotionally unmoved, prompting Anne to revise her account. Partners were likely to remember—and remind each other—how their emotions and opinions had changed over time. Contextualizing Brian's rosy memories of his participation in the weddings and his articulation of his stead-fast support of Mayor Gavin Newsom, Robert reminded Brian that he had ardently opposed Newsom's election before the weddings and was suspicious of the events even as the two participated. Interviewing couples together allowed them to correct and challenge each other on statements that I had no way of knowing might be inaccurate. More importantly, the joint interview structure actually generated data that could not have been obtained from interviewing participants individually (Allan 1980).

Some critiques have been made of joint interviewing, most saliently that it may suppress conflict and encourage interviewees to present a coherent "public" account of their experience (Cornwell 1984). In this study, however, even when interviewed together, couples did not always tell the same story. They generally agreed on the basic parameters of the experience—providing confirmation of dates, gifts received, and such—but often diverged in their accounts of why they married, what it meant to them personally, and even what they felt it meant to the relationship. For example, in my interview with Philip and Steven, Philip made it clear that he participated in the city hall weddings only because it was important to Steven. He explained, "He [Steven] wanted it so much. So I thought, okay, I better go. Didn't really matter to me." In response, Steven affirmed that the weddings were important to him and acknowledged that Philip did not feel

Name	Age	Race	Occupation	Spouse*	Time together when married (years)
Aaron	29	White	Lawyer	Gabe	6
Addy	31	White & Native American	Customer service representative	Julie	3
Alan	38	White	Construction manager	Chris	8
Anne	54	White	Artist	Lynn	11
Barbara	48	White	Electrician	Gayle	3
Brian	40	White	Attorney	Robert	11
Carrie	37	White	Social worker	Lois	2
Chris	32	Latino	Marketing manager	Alan	8
Craig	60	White	Research manager	Stanley	23
Cynthia	57	White	Federal employee	Janet	12
Dale	42	White	Nightclub manager	Pierre	3
Deirdre	37	White	Writer	Leslie	4
Diana	51	Asian American & white	Administrative assistant	Mia	8
Elizabeth	54	White	Accounting assistant	Laura	15
Ernesto	58	Latino	Health educator	Tony	28
Frank	70	White	Retired	Henry	50
Isabel	39	White	Professor	Raine	6

(continued)

Name	Age	Race	Occupation	Spouse*	Time together when married (years)
Janet	53	White	Nurse	*Cynthia*	12
Jeffrey	63	White	Retired physician	*Roger*	10
Julie	35	Middle Eastern & white	Project manager	*Addy*	3
Keith	47	White	Attorney	*Tim*	17
Kelly	39	White	Professor	*Michelle*	8
Laura	58	White	Retired	*Elizabeth*	15
Lois	42	White	Physical therapist	*Carrie*	2
Lynn	46	White	Senior center director	*Anne*	11
Marnie	57	Litvak	Accountant	*Phyllis*	25
Michelle	41	White	Accountant	*Kelly*	8
Olivia	40	Latina	Programmer	*Sandra*	4
Philip	34	Asian American & white	Project coordinator	*Steven*	3
Phoebe	37	White	Analyst	*Alex*	1.5
Pierre	43	White	Project development director	*Dale*	3
Raine	45	White	Disabled	*Isabel*	6
Robert	36	White	Physical therapist	*Brian*	11
Roger	68	White	Retired	*Jeffrey*	10

(*continued*)

TABLE A.2

RESPONDENT DEMOGRAPHICS (*continued*)

NAME	AGE	RACE	OCCUPATION	SPOUSE*	TIME TOGETHER WHEN MARRIED (YEARS)
Sandra	50	African American & Native American	Disabled	*Olivia*	4
Sonia	53	African American	Human services supervisor	Beatriz	3
Sophie	40	White	Graduate student	Lal	6
Stanley	56	White	Software engineer	*Craig*	23
Steven	39	White	Director at nonprofit	*Philip*	3
Susan	49	White	Librarian	Dawn	7
Terrance	53	African American	Retired	Jack	8
Tim	43	Asian American & white	Policy analyst	*Keith*	17

*Italicized spouses were also interviewed and are included in the table in their own row.

the same. The structure of the joint interview allowed for the differentiation of interviewees' experiences as well as the articulation of similarities in their experience.

Scholars have also pointed to the challenge of getting equal participation from both members of a couple, particularly finding in different-sex relationships that men "steal the scene" (Jordan et al. 1992) or, alternately, that women dominate (Seale et al. 2008). Although an advantage of interviewing same-sex couples is the supposed absence of gender dynamics in expectations about the appropriate speaker, in several instances one member of a couple spoke more than the other. Often, the dominating member of the couple spoke of "we" (Morris 2001; Seale et al. 2008), taking the responsibility of conveying experience and perception on behalf of the couple. I made explicit efforts to elicit responses to subjective questions from both members of the couple but did not ask the less-verbal partner to repeat couple-level information shared by his or her partner. This directed turn-taking encouraged both partners to contribute. At times, partners initiated their own turn-taking, accepting my question as theirs to answer ("I'll take this one"), directing it to their spouse ("Why don't you answer this one?"), or answering it themselves and then volleying it to their spouse for comment. I received individual responses for all key questions in the interview.

As discussed in my first chapter, I was not able to interview the partners of all respondents. Twelve participants were interviewed individually and there were a range of reasons why the second member of the couple was unavailable. I found no systematic differences in the content of the solo interviews and the joint interviews.

KEY INFORMANT INTERVIEWS

My second source of data is seven interviews with key informants. Five were activists involved in key marriage equality organizations active in the Bay Area at the time of the San Francisco weddings. I interviewed Molly McKay, founder and head of Marriage Equality USA (MEUSA) and previously of Marriage Equality California (MECA); Geoff Kors, executive director, and Seth Kilbourn, policy director, of Equality California (EQCA); Toni Broaddus, executive director of Equality Foundation (EF) and formerly the program officer at EQCA; and a former chapter head of MECA who preferred to remain anonymous. These individuals participated in the organization of the weddings and/ or the publicity and mobilization around them, and several of them (McKay, Broaddus, and the anonymous MECA chapter head) were participants themselves.

The two remaining key informant interviews were with public officials in California. I spoke with California assemblyman Mark Leno, who, with San Francisco assessor-recorder Mabel Teng, performed ninety marriage ceremonies on the first day the licenses were

issued, and with a government employee who has been key in organizing legislation on behalf of the gay and lesbian community, but who
preferred to remain anonymous and provide information "on background" since he is in a staff position and wants credit to accrue to
elected officials.

Interviews were conducted during August and September of 2007,
and all but one, with McKay, took place over the phone while the
informants were at work. The interviews ranged in length from thirty
minutes to one hour and averaged forty minutes, owing largely to
the interviewees' schedules. Despite their busy schedules, these individuals expressed great enthusiasm for my project and made themselves available. The key informant interviews were used primarily to
obtain factual information on the weddings and were not analyzed
for themes or broader patterns. Their interviews contributed greatly
to my understanding of how and why the license issuing came about.

NOTES

CHAPTER 1 — THE WINTER OF LOVE

1. President Bush made this call in response to the November 2003 ruling by the Supreme Judicial Court of Massachusetts that excluding same-sex couples from marriage violated the Massachusetts state constitution. The court directed Massachusetts to begin issuing marriage licenses to same-sex couples within 180 days. During his January 20, 2004, State of the Union address, Bush reacted to this decision, saying, "If judges insist on forcing their arbitrary will upon the people, the only alternative left to the people would be the constitutional process. Our nation must defend the sanctity of marriage" (Bush 2004).

2. For a full account of Newsom's thinking and how the weddings came about, see the film *One Wedding and a Revolution* (Chasnoff 2004).

3. Until the 1967 US Supreme Court ruling in *Loving v. Virginia,* 388 U.S. 1, 12 (1967), marriage between a man and a woman of different races was illegal in many US states. In the *Loving* decision, the court ruled these state-level laws unconstitutional.

4. I further note that scholars of marriage and family have not identified theoretically valid cut points in the experience of marriage. That is, there are no studies that find a difference in "married-ness" based on the length of time an individual or couple is married. Indeed, much of the sociological literature depends on the binary distinction between married and unmarried, without any quantification of how long married (or unmarried).

5. Although these percentages suggest keen interest in legal partnership recognition among same-sex couples, comparison to rates of marriage among different-sex couples is instructive. For the reported time frame, more than 90 percent of different-sex couples were married (Gates et al. 2008). Nonetheless, while the percentage of same-sex couples in legally recognized partnerships is on the rise, the rate of different-sex couples marrying is declining. Gates and colleagues (2008) project that the two percentages will level out to be the same in less than twenty years.

6. Specifically, Bourdieu (1984) uses the concepts of habitus, capital, and fields to argue that practice is dependent not only on historical definitions

(conveyed through habitus), but also on an individual's social power (capital) and the field of social relations in which the practice takes place. These variables intersect in different ways to produce different practices that may or may not reify existing meanings of social structures like marriage.

7. Attentive readers will note that although I use the term "same-sex" marriage throughout this book, here I am talking about gender, not sex. That is, I am analyzing the way assumptions about oppositionally situated categories of behavior, attitudes, and characteristics (that is, gender) are socially produced and contested, not how biological variation has been constructed into dichotomous categories (that is, sex). Technically speaking, these marriages are "same-gender." For the purposes of clarity in this book, however, I have deferred to the popular convention of calling it same-sex marriage. I have opted not to use the term "gay marriage" because it can elide the experience of lesbians, and the differences in the social locations of gay men and lesbians are a key analytical component of my argument.

CHAPTER 2 — MARRYING FOR THE MOVEMENT

1. City hall should not be overstated as a symbol of homophobic acts. In the years since 1978, numerous city officials, both elected and appointed, have been openly gay, and the building has not seen that kind of violent hostility to homosexuality in the ensuing years. Nonetheless, as Keith's response underscores, city hall carries a history meaningful to the struggle for gay and lesbian rights.

CHAPTER 3 — MARRYING FOR RIGHTS

1. Powell and colleagues' (2010) research on how the general public defines family underscores the key role of marriage in this social definition. For a segment of their sample, marriage and family are defined through a circular logic: "family" is defined by participation in marriage, but marriage is considered appropriate only for couples who can meet the existing definition of family. This logic operates to exclude same-sex couples, both with children and childfree, from the definition of family in areas that do not permit same-sex marriage.

2. There are no reliable figures on the number of second-parent adoptions in lesbian and gay households. Using data from the early 2000s, Gates and colleagues (2007) estimate the presence of approximately fifty-two thousand legally adopted children under eighteen in households with same-sex parents, a figure that includes second-parent adoptions as well as public, private, and international adoptions.

3. Isabel was referring to pop stars Britney Spears and Jennifer Lopez. Spears married Jason Alexander on January 3, 2004, and then had the marriage

annulled fifty-five hours later. Lopez had been married three times at the time of the interview.

CHAPTER 7 — EXPOSING HETERONORMATIVITY

1. Respondents did not distinguish among the effects of the wedding ceremony, the lived experience of being married, and the emotional experience of the license invalidation in discussing how their experience affected their lives, including their participation in activism. This is likely an effect of my interviewing them over a year and a half after the license invalidation. It does seem logical that each had distinct impacts, especially given the emotions they discussed in response to different parts of their overall marriage experience, but I am unable to explore that possibility.

REFERENCES

Adam, Barry D. 2004. "Care, Intimacy, and Same-Sex Partnership in the 21st Century." *Current Sociology* 52:265–279.

Allan, G. 1980. "A Note on Interviewing Spouses Together." *Journal of Marriage and the Family* 42:205–210.

Alm, James, M. V. Lee Badgett, and Leslie A. Whittington. 2000. "Wedding Bell Blues: The Income Tax Consequences of Legalizing Same-Sex Marriage." *National Tax Journal* 53:201–214.

Altman, Dennis. 1979. *Coming Out in the Seventies.* Sydney, Australia: Wild & Wooley.

Arksey, Hilary. 1996. "Collecting Data through Joint Interviews." *Social Research Update* 15:1–4.

Armstrong, Elizabeth A. 2002. *Forging Gay Identities: Organizing Sexuality in San Francisco, 1950–1994.* Chicago: University of Chicago Press.

Arnett, Jeffrey Jensen. 2004. *Emerging Adulthood: The Winding Road from the Late Teens through the Twenties.* New York: Oxford University Press.

Auchmuty, Rosemary. 2004. "Same-Sex Marriage Revived: Feminist Critique and Legal Strategy." *Feminism & Psychology* 14:101–126.

Avellar, Sarah, and Pamela Smock. 2003. "Has the Price of Motherhood Declined over Time? A Cross-Cohort Comparison of the Motherhood Wage Penalty." *Journal of Marriage and the Family* 65:597–607.

Badgett, M. V. Lee. 2001. *Money, Myths, and Change: The Economic Lives of Lesbians and Gay Men.* Chicago: University of Chicago Press.

———. 2009. *When Gay People Get Married: What Happens When Societies Legalize Same-Sex Marriage.* New York: New York University Press.

Badgett, M. V. Lee, and Jody L. Herman. 2011. "Patterns of Relationship Recognition by Same-Sex Couples in the United States." Report for the Williams Institute, University of California, Los Angeles.

Bellah, Robert N., Richard Madsen, William M. Sullivan, Ann Swidler, and Steven M. Tipton. 2008. *Habits of the Heart: Individualism and Commitment in American Life.* Berkeley: University of California Press. First published 1985.

Bennett, Lisa, and Gary Gates. 2004. "The Cost of Marriage Inequality to Children and Their Same-Sex Parents." Report for the Human Rights Campaign Foundation, Washington, DC.

Berkowitz, Dana. 2009. "Theorizing Lesbian and Gay Parenting: Past, Present, and Future Scholarship." *Journal of Family Theory and Review* 1:117–132.

Bernstein, Mary. 1997. "Celebration and Suppression: The Strategic Uses of Identity by the Lesbian and Gay Movement." *American Journal of Sociology* 103:531–565.

———. 2001. "Gender Transgressions and Queer Family Law: Gender, Queer Family Policies, and the Limits of Law." In *Queer Families, Queer Politics: Challenging Culture and the State,* edited by M. Bernstein and R. Reimann, 420–446. New York: Columbia University Press.

Bernstein, Mary, and Verta Taylor. 2013a. "Marital Discord: Understanding the Contested Place of Marriage in the Lesbian and Gay Movement." In *The Marrying Kind: Debating Same-Sex Marriage within the Lesbian and Gay Movement,* edited by M. Bernstein and V. Taylor, 1–35. Minneapolis: University of Minnesota Press.

———. eds. 2013b. *The Marrying Kind? Debating Same-Sex Marriage within the Lesbian and Gay Movement.* Minneapolis: University of Minnesota Press.

Berzon, Betty. 1979. "Telling the Family You're Gay." In *Positively Gay,* edited by B. Berzon and R. Leighton, 88–100. Los Angeles: Mediamix Associates.

Best, Amy L. 2000. *Prom Night: Youth, Schools, and Popular Culture.* New York: Routledge.

Blumstein, Philip, and Pepper Schwartz. 1983. *American Couples: Money, Work, Sex.* New York: William Morrow & Co.

Bourdieu, Pierre. 1977. *Outline of a Theory of Practice.* Translated by R. Nice. New York: Cambridge University Press.

———. 1984. *Distinction: A Social Critique of the Judgment of Taste.* Translated by R. Nice. Cambridge, MA: Harvard University Press.

———. 1998. *Practical Reason: On the Theory of Action.* Stanford, CA: Stanford University Press.

———. 2001. "The Forms of Capital." In *The Sociology of Economic Life,* edited by M. Granovetter and R. Swedberg, 96–111. Cambridge, MA: Westview Press.

Bourdieu, Pierre, and Loic J. D. Wacquant. 1992. *An Invitation to Reflexive Sociology.* Chicago: University of Chicago Press.

Britt, Lory, and David Heise. 2000. "From Shame to Pride in Identity Politics." In *Self, Identity, and Social Movements,* edited by S. Stryker, T. J. Owens, and R. W. White, 252–270. Minneapolis: University of Minnesota Press.

Budig, Michelle J., and Paula England. 2001. "The Wage Penalty for Motherhood." *American Sociological Review* 66:204–225.

Bunch, Charlotte. 1987. *Passionate Politics: Essays 1968–1986: Feminist Theory in Action.* New York: St. Martin's Press.

Burgess, Ernest W., and Harvey J. Locke. 1945. *The Family: From Institution to Companionship.* New York: American Book.

Bush, George W. 2004. "State of the Union Address." Accessed November 4, 2010. http://www.c-span.org/executive/transcript.asp.

Butler, Judith. 2002. "Is Kinship Always Already Heterosexual?" *differences* 13:14–44.

———. 2005. *Undoing Gender.* New York: Routledge.

Calhoun, Cheshire. 2000. *Feminism, the Family, and the Politics of the Closet: Lesbian and Gay Displacement.* Oxford: Oxford University Press.

Chambers, David L. 2001. "What If? The Legal Consequences of Marriage and the Legal Needs of Lesbian and Gay Male Couples." In *Queer Families, Queer Politics: Challenging Culture and the State,* edited by M. Bernstein and R. Reimann, 306–337. Minneapolis: University of Minnesota Press.

Chan, Raymond W., Risa C. Brooks, Barbara Raboy, and Charlotte J. Patterson. 1998. "Division of Labor among Lesbian and Heterosexual Parents: Association with Children's Development." *Journal of Family Psychology* 12:402–419.

Chasnoff, Debra. 2004. *One Wedding and a Revolution* (film). 19 minutes. Women's Educational Media, San Francisco, CA.

Chauncey, George. 2004. *Why Marriage? The History Shaping Today's Debate over Gay Equality.* New York: Basic Books.

Cherlin, Andrew. 2004. "The Deinstitutionalization of Marriage." *Journal of Marriage and the Family* 66:848–861.

———. 2009. *The Marriage-Go-Round: The State of Marriage and the Family in America Today.* New York: Vintage Books.

Clarke, Victoria. 2002. "Resistance and Normalisation in the Construction of Lesbian and Gay Families: A Discursive Analysis." In *Lesbian and Gay Psychology: New Perspectives,* edited by A. Coyle and C. Kitzinger, 98–118. Oxford: Blackwell.

Cohen, Philip N. 2002. "Cohabitation and the Declining Marriage Premium for Men." *Work and Occupations* 29:326–363.

Cohn, D'Vera, Jeffrey S. Passell, and Wendy Wang. 2011. "Barely Half of U.S. Adults Are Married—A Record Low." Pew Social and Demographic Trends, Pew Research Center, Washington, DC.

Collins, Patricia Hill. 2005. *Black Sexual Politics: African Americans, Gender, and the New Racism.* New York: Routledge.

Connell, Raewyn. 2009. "Accountable Conduct: 'Doing Gender' in Transsexual and Political Retrospect." *Gender & Society* 23:104–111.

Coontz, Stephanie. 2004. "The World Historical Transformation of Marriage." *Journal of Marriage and the Family* 66:947–979.

————. 2005. *Marriage, a History: From Obedience to Intimacy, or How Love Conquered Marriage.* New York: Viking.

Cornwell, J. 1984. *Hard-Earned Lives: Accounts of Health and Illness from East London.* London: Tavistock.

Cott, Nancy F. 2000. *Public Vows: A History of Marriage and the Nation.* Cambridge, MA: Harvard University Press.

Dalton, Susan. 2001. "Protecting Our Parent-Child Relationships: Understanding the Strengths and Weaknesses of Second-Parent Adoption." In *Queer Families, Queer Politics: Challenging Culture and the State,* edited by M. Bernstein and R. Reimann, 201–220. Minneapolis: University of Minnesota Press.

de Vries, Brian. 2007. "LGBT Couples in Later Life: A Study in Diversity." *Generations* 32:75–80.

de Vries, Brian, Anne M. Mason, Jean Quam, and Kimberly Acquaviva. 2009. "State Recognition of Same-Sex Relationships and Preparation for End of Life among Lesbian and Gay Boomers." *Sexuality Research and Social Policy* 6:90–101.

Dryden, Caroline. 1999. *Being Married, Doing Gender: A Critical Analysis of Gender Relationships in Marriage.* New York: Routledge.

Duggan, Lisa. 2003. *The Twilight of Equality? Neoliberalism, Cultural Politics, and the Attack on Democracy.* Boston: Beacon Press.

Echols, Alice. 1989. *Daring to Be Bad: Radical Feminism in America, 1967–1975.* Minneapolis: University of Minnesota Press.

Edgell, Stephen. 1980. *Middle-Class Couples: A Study of Segregation, Domination, and Inequality in Marriage.* London: G. Allen & Unwin.

Epstein, Steven. 1996. *Impure Science: AIDS, Activism, and the Politics of Knowledge.* Berkeley: University of California Press.

Eskridge, William N., Jr. 1993. "A History of Same-Sex Marriage." *Virginia Law Review* 79:1419–1513.

————. 2002. *Equality Practice: Civil Unions and the Future of Gay Rights.* New York: Routledge.

Eskridge, William N., Jr., and Darren Spedale. 2006. *Gay Marriage: For Better or for Worse? What We've Learned from the Evidence.* Oxford: Oxford University Press.

Ettelbrick, Paula L. 1992. "Since When Is Marriage a Path to Liberation?" In *Lesbian and Gay Marriage: Private Commitments, Public Ceremonies,* edited by S. Sherman, 20–26. Philadelphia: Temple University Press.

Fetner, Tina. 2008. *How the Religious Right Shaped Lesbian and Gay Activism.* Minneapolis: University of Minnesota Press.

Fields, J. 2001. "Normal Queers: Straight Parents Respond to Their Children's 'Coming Out.'" *Symbolic Interaction* 24:165–187.

Finch, Janet. 2007. "Displaying Families." *Sociology* 41:65–81.

Finlay, Sara-Jane, and Victoria Clarke. 2003. "'A Marriage of Inconvenience?' Feminist Perspectives on Marriage." *Feminism & Psychology* 13:415–420.

Foucault, Michel. 1978. *The History of Sexuality: An Introduction.* Translated by R. Hurley. New York: Pantheon Books.

Franklin, Sarah. 1993. "Essentialism, Which Essentialism? Some Implications of Reproductive and Genetic Techno-Science." *Journal of Homosexuality* 24:27–40.

Garnets, Linda D., and Douglas C. Kimmel. 1993. "Lesbian and Gay Male Dimensions in the Psychological Study of Human Diversity." In *Psychological Perspectives on Lesbian and Gay Male Experiences,* edited by L. D. Garnets and D. C. Kimmel, 1–51. New York: Columbia University Press.

Gates, Gary, M. V. Lee Badgett, and Deborah Ho. 2008. "Marriage, Registration, and Dissolution by Same-Sex Couples in the U.S." Report for the Williams Institute, University of Californis, Los Angeles.

Gates, Gary, M. V. Lee Badgett, Jennifer Ehrle Macomber, and Kate Chambers. 2007. "Adoption and Foster Care by Gay and Lesbian Parents in the United States." Report for the Williams Institute and the Urban Institute, University of Californis, Los Angeles.

Geller, Jaclyn. 2001. *Here Comes the Bride: Women, Weddings, and the Marriage Mystique.* New York: Four Walls Eight Windows.

General Accounting Office. 2004. "Defense of Marriage Act: Update to Prior Report." Accessed July 23, 2007. http://www.gao.gov/new.items/d04353r .pdf.

Ghaziani, Amin. 2008. *The Dividends of Dissent: How Conflict and Culture Work in Lesbian and Gay Marches on Washington.* Chicago: University of Chicago Press.

———. 2011. "Post-Gay Collective Identity Construction." *Social Problems* 58:99–125.

Giddens, Anthony. 1991. *Modernity and Self-Identity.* Stanford, CA: Stanford University Press.

Glauber, Rebecca. 2007. "Marriage and the Motherhood Wage Penalty among African Americans, Hispanics, and Whites." *Journal of Marriage and the Family* 69:951–961.

———. 2008. "Race and Gender in Families and at Work: The Fatherhood Wage Premium." *Gender & Society* 22:8–30.

Green, Adam Isaiah. 2006. "Until Death Do Us Part? The Impact of Differential Access to Marriage on a Sample of Urban Men." *Social Perspectives* 49:163–189.

———. 2010. "Queer Unions: Same-Sex Spouses Marrying Tradition and Innovation." *Canadian Journal of Sociology* 35:399–436.

Hagan, K. L. 1993. *Fugitive Information: Essays from a Feminist Hothead.* New York: Harper Collins.

Heath, Melanie. 2009. "State of Our Unions: Marriage Promotion and the Contested Power of Heterosexuality." *Gender & Society* 23:27–48.

Herdt, Gilbert, and Robert Kertzner. 2006. "I Do, but I Can't: The Impact of Marriage Denial on the Mental Health and Sexual Citizenship of Lesbians and Gay Men in the United States." *Sexuality Research and Social Policy* 3:33–49.

Howard, Vicki. 2006. *Brides, Inc.: American Weddings and the Business of Tradition.* Philadelphia: University of Pennsylvania Press.

Hull, Kathleen E. 2006. *Same-Sex Marriage: The Cultural Politics of Love and Law.* Cambridge: Cambridge University Press.

Hunt, Mary E. 2003. "Same-Sex Marriage and Relational Justice." *Journal of Feminist Studies in Religion* 20:83–92.

Hunter, Nan. 1995. "Marriage, Law, and Gender: A Feminist Inquiry." In *Sex Wars: Sexual Dissent and Political Culture,* edited by L. Duggan and N. Hunter, 105–118. New York: Routledge.

Infanti, Anthony C. 2007. *Everyday Law for Gays and Lesbians and Those Who Care about Them.* Boulder, CO: Paradigm Publishers.

Ingraham, Chrys. 1994. "The Heterosexual Imaginary: Feminist Sociology and Theories of Gender." *Sociological Theory* 12:203–219.

———. 1999. *White Weddings: Romancing Heterosexuality in Popular Culture.* New York: Routledge.

———. 2003. "Ritualizing Heterosexuality: Weddings as Performance." In *Sexual Lives: A Reader on the Theories and Realities of Human Sexualities,* edited by R. Heasley and B. Crane, 235–245. New York: McGraw Hill.

———. 2005a. "Introduction: Thinking Straight." In *Thinking Straight: The Power, the Promise, and the Paradox of Heterosexuality,* edited by C. Ingraham, 1–14. New York: Routledge.

———. ed. 2005b. *Thinking Straight: The Power, the Promise, and the Paradox of Heterosexuality.* New York: Routledge.

Jaggar, A. M. 1994. *Living with Contradictions: Controversies in Feminist Social Ethics.* Boulder, CO: Westview Press.

Jeffreys, Sheila. 2004. "The Need to Abolish Marriage." *Feminism & Psychology* 14:327–331.

Jordan, B., S. James, H. Kay, and M. Redley. 1992. *Trapped in Poverty? Labour-Market Decisions in Low-Income Households.* London: Routledge.

Josephson, Jyl J. 2005. "Citizenship, Same-Sex Marriage, and Feminist Critiques of Marriage." *Perspectives on Politics* 3:269–284.

Kandaswamy, Priya. 2008. "State Austerity and the Racial Politics of Same-Sex Marriage in the US." *Sexualities* 11:706–725.

Kimport, Katrina. 2012. "Remaking the White Wedding? Same-Sex Wedding Photographs' Challenge to Symbolic Heteronormativity." *Gender & Society* 26:874–898.

Kitzinger, Celia, and Sue Wilkinson. 2004. "Social Advocacy for Equal Marriage: The Politics of 'Rights' and the Psychology of 'Mental Health.'" *Analyses of Social Issues and Public Policy* 4:173–194.

Korenman, Sanders, and David Neumark. 1991. "Does Marriage Really Make Men More Productive?" *Journal of Human Resources* 26:282–307.

Kotulski, Davina. 2004. *Why You Should Give a Damn about Gay Marriage*. Los Angeles: Advocate Books.

Kurdek, Lawrence A. 1993. "The Allocation of Household Labor in Gay, Lesbian, and Heterosexual Married Couples." *Journal of Social Issues* 49:127–139.

———. 1995. "Lesbian and Gay Couples." In *Lesbian, Gay, and Bisexual Identities over the Lifespan: Psychological Perspectives,* edited by A. R. D'Augelli and C. J. Patterson, 243–261. New York: Oxford University Press.

Lahey, Kathleen A., and Kevin Alderson. 2004. *Same-Sex Marriage: The Personal and the Political.* Toronto, Ontario, Canada: Insomniac Press.

Lane, Julie D., and Daniel M. Wegner. 1995. "The Cognitive Consequences of Secrecy." *Journal of Personality and Social Psychology* 69:237–254.

Langford, Wendy. 1999. *Revolutions of the Heart: Gender, Power, and the Delusions of Love.* New York: Routledge.

Lewin, Ellen. 1993. *Lesbian Mothers: Accounts of Gender in American Culture.* Ithaca, NY: Cornell University Press.

———. 1998. *Recognizing Ourselves: Ceremonies of Lesbian and Gay Commitment.* New York: Columbia University Press.

Lofton, Katie, and Donald P. Haider-Markel. 2007. "The Politics of Same-Sex Marriage versus the Politics of Gay Civil Rights: A Comparison of Public Opinion and State Voting Patterns." In *The Politics of Same-Sex Marriage,* edited by C. A. Rimmerman and C. Wilcox, 313–340. Chicago: University of Chicago Press.

Loh, Eng Seng. 1996. "Productivity Differences and the Marriage Wage Premiuim for White Males." *Journal of Human Resources* 31:566–589.

Mamo, Laura. 2007. *Queering Reproduction: Achieving Pregnancy in the Age of Technology.* Durham, NC: Duke University Press.

Martin, Karin A. 2009. "Normalizing Heterosexuality: Mothers' Assumptions, Talk, and Strategies with Young Children." *American Sociological Review* 74:190–207.

Martin, Karin A., and Emily Kazyak. 2009. "Hetero-Romantic Love and Heterosexiness in Children's G-Rated Films." *Gender & Society* 23:315–336.

Mason, Jennifer. 1989. "Reconstructing the Public and the Private: The Home and Marriage in Later Life." In *Home and Family: Creating the Domestic Sphere,* edited by G. Allan and G. Crow, 102–121. London: MacMillan.

Mays, Vicki M., and Susan D. Cochran. 2001. "Mental Health Correlates of Perceived Discrimination among Lesbian, Gay, and Bisexual Adults in the United States." *American Journal of Public Health* 91:1869–1876.

182 REFERENCES

McKee, Lorna, and Margaret O'Brien. 1983. "Interviewing Men: 'Taking Gender Seriously.'" In *The Public and the Private*, edited by E. Gamarnikow, D.H.J. Morgan, J. Purvis, and D. Taylorson, 147–159. London: Heinemann.

McKinney, Kevin. 1987. "How to Become a Gay Father." *The Advocate*, December 8, 52–55.

Mezey, Nancy J. 2008. *New Choices, New Families: How Lesbians Decide about Motherhood*. Baltimore: The Johns Hopkins University Press.

Morris, Sara M. 2001. "Joint and Individual Interviewing in the Context of Cancer." *Qualitative Health Research* 11:553–567.

Murphy, Julien S. 2001. "Should Lesbians Count as Infertile Couples? Antilesbian Discrimination in Assisted Reproduction." In *Queer Families, Queer Politics: Challenging Culture and the State*, edited by M. Bernstein and R. Reimann, 182–200. Minneapolis: University of Minnesota Press.

Murphy, Tim. 2011. "Ready to Wed? No, Mom." *New York Times, July 22.*

Ocobock, Abigail. 2013. "The Power and Limits of Marriage: Married Gay Men's Family Relationships." Journal of Marriage and Family 75:191–205.

Oswald, Ramona Faith. 2000. "A Member of the Wedding? Heterosexism and Family Ritual." *Journal of Social and Personal Relationships* 17:349–368.

Otnes, Cele C., and Elizabeth H. Pleck. 2003. *Cinderella Dreams: The Allure of the Lavish Wedding*. Berkeley: University of California Press.

Patterson, Charlotte J., Erin L. Sutfin, and Megan Fulcher. 2004. "Division of Labor among Lesbian and Heterosexual Parenting Couples: Correlates of Specialized versus Shared Patterns." *Journal of Adult Development* 11:179–189

Pinello, Daniel R. 2006. *American's Struggle for Same-Sex Marriage*. Cambridge: Cambridge University Press.

Plummer, Ken. 1995. *Telling Sexual Stories: Power, Change, and Social Worlds*. New York: Routledge.

Polikoff, Nancy. 2008. *Beyond Straight and Gay Marriage: Valuing All Families under the Law*. Boston: Beacon Press.

Porter, Maureen, and Siladitya Bhattacharya. 2008. "Helping Themselves to Get Pregnant: A Qualitative Longitudinal Study on the Information-Seeking Behaviour of Infertile Couples." *Human Reproduction* 23:567–572.

Powell, Brian, Catherine Bolzendahl, Claudia Geist, and Lala Carr Steelman. 2010. *Counted Out: Same-Sex Relations and Americans' Definitions of Family*. New York: Russell Sage Foundation.

Rauch, Jonathan. 2004. *Gay Marriage: Why It Is Good for Gays, Good for Straights, and Good for America*. New York: Times Books/Henry Holt and Co.

Rich, Adrienne. 1980. "Compulsory Heterosexuality and Lesbian Existence." *Signs* 5:631–660.

Richardson, Diane. 1996. "Heterosexuality and Social Theory." In *Theorizing Heterosexuality: Telling it Straight,* edited by D. Richardson, 1–20. Buckingham: Open University Press.

———. 2003. "Heterosexuality and Social Theory." In *Sexual Lives: A Reader on the Theories and Realities of Human Sexualities,* edited by R. Heasley and B. Crane, 371–387. New York: McGraw Hill.

Riggle, Ellen D. B., and Sharon S. Rostosky. 2007. "The Consequences of Marriage Policy for Same-Sex Couples' Well-Being." In *The Politics of Same-Sex Marriage,* edited by C. A. Rimmerman and C. Wilcox, 65–84. Chicago: University of Chicago Press.

Robinson, V. 1997. "My Baby Just Cares for Me: Feminism, Heterosexuality, and Non-monogamy." *Journal of Gender Studies* 6:143–157.

Rosa, B. 1994. "Anti-monogamy: A Radical Challenge to Compulsory Heterosexuality." In *Stirring It: Challenges for Feminism,* edited by G. Griffin, M. Hester, S. Rai, and S. Roseneil, 107–120. London: Taylor and Francis.

Rupp, Leila J., and Verta Taylor. 2003. *Drag Queens at the 801 Cabaret.* Chicago: University of Chicago Press.

Rydstrom, Jens. 2011. *Odd Couples: A History of Gay Marriage in Scandinavia.* Amersterdam: Amsterdam University Press.

Savin-Williams, Ritch C., and Richard G. Rodriguez. 1993. "A Developmental, Clinical Perspective on Lesbian, Gay Male, and Bisexual Youths." In *Adolescent Sexuality: Advances in Adolescent Development,* edited by T. P. Gullota, G. R. Adams, and R. Montemayor, 176–205. Thousand Oaks, CA: Sage.

Seale, Clive, Jonathan Charteris-Black, Carol Dumelow, Louise Locock, and Sue Ziebland. 2008. "The Effects of Joint Interviewing on the Performance of Gender." *Field Methods* 20:107–128.

Sennett, Richard, and Jonathan Cobb. 1972. *The Hidden Injuries of Class.* New York: Alfred A. Knopf.

Seymour, Julie, Gill Dix, and Tony Eardley. 1995. *Joint Accounts: Methodology and Practice in Research Interviews with Couples.* York, UK: University of York Social Policy Research Unit.

Sherman, Suzanne. 1992. "Lesbian and Gay Marriage: Private Commitments, Public Ceremonies." Philadelphia: Temple University Press.

Simmons, Tavia, and Martin O'Connell. 2003. "Married-Couple and Unmarried-Partner Households: 2000." *Census 2000 Special Reports.* Washington, DC: US Census Bureau.

Solomon, Sondra E., Esther D. Rothblum, and Kimberly F. Balsam. 2004. "Pioneers in Partnership: Lesbian and Gay Male Couples in Civil Unions Compared with Those Not in Civil Unions and Married Heterosexual Siblings." *Journal of Family Psychology* 18:275–286.

Stacey, Judith. 2004. "Cruising to Familyland: Gay Hypergamy and Rainbow Kinship." *Current Sociology* 52:181–197.

Stacey, Judith, and T. J. Biblarz. 2001. "(How) Does the Sexual Orientation of Parents Matter?" *American Sociological Review* 66:159–183.

Star, Jack. 1971. "The Homosexual Couple." *Look*, January 26, 69.

Stein, Arlene. 1997. *Sex and Sensibility: Stories of a Lesbian Generation.* Berkeley: University of California Press.

Stelboum, J. P. 1999. "Patriarchal Monogamy." In *The Lesbian Polyamory Reader*, edited by M. Munson and J. P. Stelboum, 39–46. New York: Haworth Press.

Stokes, Mason. 2005. "White Heterosexuality: A Romance of the Straight Man's Burden." In *Thinking Straight: The Power, the Promise, and the Paradox of Heterosexuality*, edited by C. Ingraham, 131–149. New York: Routledge.

Sullivan, Andrew. 1997. Introduction to *Same-Sex Marriage: Pro and Con*, edited by A. Sullivan, xvii–xxvi. New York: Vintage Books.

Sullivan, Maureen. 2004. *The Family of Woman: Lesbian Mothers, Their Children, and the Undoing of Gender.* Berkeley: University of California Press.

Swidler, Ann. 1986. "Culture in Action: Symbols and Strategies." *American Sociological Review* 51:273–286.

———. 2001. *Talk of Love: How Culture Matters.* Chicago: University of Chicago Press.

Taylor, Verta, and Kathleen Blee. 2002. "Semi-structured Interviewing in Social Movement Research." In *Methods of Social Movement Research*, edited by B. Klandermans and S. Staggenborg, 92–117. Minneapolis: University of Minnesota Press.

Taylor, Verta, Katrina Kimport, Nella Van Dyke, and Ellen Ann Andersen. 2009. "Culture and Mobilization: Tactical Repertoires, Same-Sex Weddings, and the Impact on Gay Activism." *American Sociological Review* 74:865–890.

Taylor, Verta, and Leila J. Rupp. 2005. "When the Girls Are Men: Negotiating Gender and Sexual Dynamics in a Study of Drag Queens." *Signs* 30:2155–2139.

Taylor, Verta, and Nancy Whittier. 1992. "Collective Identity in Social Movement Communities: Lesbian Feminist Mobilization." In *Frontiers in Social Movement Theory*, edited by A. Morris and C. Mueller, 104–129. New Haven, CT: Yale University Press.

———. 1995. "Analytical Approaches to Social Movement Culture: The Culture of the Women's Movement." In *Social Movements and Culture*, edited by H. Johnston and B. Klandermans, 163–187. Minneapolis: University of Minnesota Press.

Teng, Mabel. 2004. "Demographics Breakdown of Same Gender Marriage." Accessed August 9, 2006. www.alicebtoklas.org/abt/samesexmarriagestats .ppt.

Valverde, Mariana. 2006. "A New Entity in the History of Sexuality: The Respectable Same-Sex Couple." *Feminist Studies* 32:155–162.

Waldfogel, Jane. 1997. "The Effect of Children on Women's Wages." *American Sociological Review* 93:659–687.

Walters, Suzanna Danuta. 2001. "Take My Domestic Partner, Please: Gays and Marriage in the Era of the Visible." In *Queer Families, Queer Politics: Challenging Culture and the State,* edited by M. Bernstein and R. Reimann, 338–357. Minneapolis: University of Minnesota Press.

Weeks, Jeffrey. 2008. "Regulation, Resistance, Recognition." *Sexualities* 11:787–792.

Weeks, Jeffrey, Brian Heaphy, and Catherine Donovan. 2001. *Same Sex Intimacies: Families of Choice and Other Life Experiments.* New York: Routledge.

Weston, Kath. 1991. *Families We Choose: Lesbians, Gays, Kinship.* New York: Columbia University Press.

Wolfson, Evan. 2004. *Why Marriage Matters: America, Equality, and Gay People's Right to Marry.* New York: Simon & Schuster.

Yep, Gust A. 2003. "The Violence of Heteronormativity in Communication Studies: Notes on Injury, Healing, and Queer World-Making." *Journal of Homosexuality* 45:11–59.

INDEX

The letter f following a page number denotes a figure. The letter t denotes a table.

ABOUT THE AUTHOR

KATRINA KIMPORT is an assistant professor in the Department of Obstetrics, Gynecology, and Reproductive Sciences and a research sociologist with the Advancing New Standards in Reproductive Health (ANSIRH) program of the Bixby Center for Global Reproductive Health at the University of California, San Francisco. Her research examines the (re)production of social inequality, with a particular focus on gender and sexuality-based inequality.

CPSIA information can be obtained at www.ICGtesting.com
Printed in the USA
BVOW01s0024141013

333571BV00002B/2/P